NO MOON AS WITNESS

NO MOON AS WITNESS

Missions of the SOE and OSS in World War II

JAMES STEJSKAL

CASEMATE
Philadelphia & Oxford

Published in the United States of America and Great Britain in 2021 by
CASEMATE PUBLISHERS
1950 Lawrence Road, Havertown, PA 19083, US
and
The Old Music Hall, 106–108 Cowley Road, Oxford OX4 1JE, UK

Copyright 2021 © James Stejskal

Hardback Edition: ISBN 978-1-61200-952-0
Digital Edition: ISBN 978-1-61200-953-7

A CIP record for this book is available from the British Library

Printed and bound in the United Kingdom by TJ Books

Typeset by Versatile PreMedia Services (P) Ltd.

For a complete list of Casemate titles, please contact:

CASEMATE PUBLISHERS (US)
Telephone (610) 853-9131
Fax (610) 853-9146
Email: casemate@casematepublishers.com
www.casematepublishers.com

CASEMATE PUBLISHERS (UK)
Telephone (01865) 241249
Email: casemate-uk@casematepublishers.co.uk
www.casematepublishers.co.uk

Dedicated to the courage and sacrifice of the men and women who served, as well as the patriots of the resistance groups with whom they fought and died.

The life that I have
Is all that I have
And the life that I have
Is yours

The love that I have
Of the life that I have
Is yours and yours and yours

A sleep I shall have
A rest I shall have
Yet death will be but a pause

For the peace of my years
In the long green grass
Will be yours and yours
and yours

SOE agent Violette Szabo, GC, used these lines as a code poem on her second and final mission. It was written by Leo Marks, a SOE cryptographer, after he learned of the death of his fiancée. He provided it to Szabo, but did not tell her of its origin.

Leo Marks, *Between Silk and Cyanide*
(London: Harper Collins, 1998)

Contents

Introduction

The Special Operations Executive (SOE) and Office of Strategic Services (OSS) were created to fight an unconventional war at a time when the normal means to bring the fight to the enemy were lacking.

At the beginning of World War II, Britain faced a fearsome wartime aggressor – the Axis alliance of Germany, Italy and later Japan – and realised it had a need for special units to do things their regular military could not. That need was to oppose the Axis indirectly in unexpected places, behind enemy lines and on the periphery until its military was ready and able to fight a conventional war.

The United States would join in the fray nearly two years later. As was quite often the case with innovations in the early 20th century, the British created their Special Operations Executive first. The Americans would follow with the Office of Strategic Services in 1942.

In sum, both SOE and OSS were conceived to fight an unconventional or subversive war – some would say a 'dirty' war – against the Germans. While SOE was essentially the action arm of British intelligence (albeit separate of the Secret Intelligence Service), OSS would serve both roles, intelligence and special operations, for the duration of the war.

From the outset, the two organisations were distrustful of each other and often demeaned their partner's capabilities before they had even met. SOE operatives regarded the Americans as inexperienced, while the American OSS often saw the British as arrogant. Differing views on the political aspects of the war added to the distrust. But the distrust each organisation had for each other was probably no worse than the issues they had with their own militaries and diplomatic services. Nevertheless, once they realised they were on the same side they banded together well to fight their common enemies.

In 1938, Europe was still traumatised by the horrific losses of sons, fathers and husbands – the so-called 'lost generation' – in World War I. Most sane people wished nothing more than to avoid another war. Among these were British and French Prime Ministers Neville Chamberlain and Edouard Daladier – honourable but short-sighted men – who thought they could negotiate a lasting peace with Germany.

But a few far-sighted leaders saw the futility of diplomacy with Adolf Hitler, the self-appointed 'messiah' of Germany. At the same time, Japan's militancy in the Far East, as well as Italy's aggression in Africa, demonstrated those countries' expansionist aims. The prospects of conflict elevated and muted alarm bells began to ring in London, Paris and finally Washington. In London there were men like Stewart Menzies, Hugh Dalton, Colin Gubbins and, of course, Winston Churchill, who realised the gloves would have to come off. In Washington, which did not have Britain's recent experiences with revolutionary uprisings like those in Ireland, Palestine or India, there were fewer who saw the role that intelligence and 'irregular' operations would serve in the coming war. Among those who did understand the need were special men: Frank Knox, William Donovan and Franklin Roosevelt.

Once both countries had adopted the concept, the two organisations developed at a rapid pace, largely due to the dynamism of the chosen directors, Hugh Dalton for SOE and William Donovan for OSS, and their abilities to work around government stove-piping.

Although the ranks of SOE and OSS were initially filled with Britons and Americans – many of them expatriates from the target countries – Frenchmen, Belgians, Norwegians, Poles and other nationalities were quickly recruited to meet the requirement for men and women who could operate clandestinely in their home countries. Soon these unconventional warriors would be in harm's way, parachuting into hostile territory at night, wading ashore onto remote beaches or crossing mountain frontiers to join the fight with the resistance against the Axis armies.

Until the end of the war in 1945, these two secret units would contribute much to the fight, and as many as 25 per cent of their operatives were killed in combat or executed after their capture. Some were sent to their deaths in concentration camps.

The history of SOE and OSS would take years to be told, and many stories remain secret. David Stafford, a historian of SOE, wrote in 1982: 'The obsession with secrecy is perhaps the true English disease.' That is still very much the case. The story of the OSS is easier to tell because its history was more completely recorded, catalogued and eventually declassified. In fact, the OSS is the only intelligence agency of any nation to have its records fully open to public inspection. Much of SOE's files and history were absorbed into the SIS after World War II and little has been revealed. Other than personnel files (and not all of them at that) and some operational details, the official record is scant. SIS is notoriously reluctant to share its secrets, even its old ones.

Previous books on the SOE, specifically M. R. D. Foot's *SOE, An Outline History* and *SOE in France* and William Mackenzie's *The Secret History of SOE*, provided much of the British story, while the *War Report of the OSS, Volumes 1 and 2* along with Aaron Linderman's *Reclaiming the Ungentlemanly Arts* and John Chambers's works on the OSS for the US Park Service informed much of the US side of things.

This work is a short history – an overview that is not intended to replace the books I've mentioned. It is a very encapsulated view of both SOE and OSS and their missions. Their histories are closely tied to one another and, with this book, I hope to show the parallels in both as well as how they worked together, and sometimes how they didn't.

Timeline

30 January 1933	Hitler becomes *Reichskanzler* of Germany
March 1938	Foreign Office set up Elektra House (EH) propaganda unit
12 March 1938	*Anschluß* – Hitler annexes Austria
April 1938	SIS (MI6) creates Section D
October 1938	GS(R) – later renamed MI(R) – created in War Office
1 September 1939	Germany invades Poland
1 September 1939	Section D moves to Frythe, near Welwyn, Hertfordshire
April–June 1940	Independent Companies under Colin Gubbins operate in Norway
May 1940	British Security Coordination office established in New York
10 May 1940	Winston Churchill becomes Prime Minister
22 June 1940	France surrenders
June–July 1940	'Wild Bill' Donovan's first survey trip to Britain
July 1940	First meeting between 'Intrepid' and 'Wild Bill'
July 1940	General Headquarters Auxiliary Units created for UK Home Defence

22 July 1940	SOE Charter approved, formed from Section D, MI(R) and EH
28 August 1940	Sir Frank Nelson appointed 'CD' – head of SOE
October 1940	Italy invades Crete, Germany follows in April 1941
November 1940	Gubbins returns to SOE as Director of Training and Operations
December 1940	Donovan begins second trip to Britain, Mediterranean and Balkans; returns February 1941
5 May 1941	First successful SOE infiltration into France; George Bégué sets up circuit and meets follow-on agents
20 May 1941	Germany invades Crete
11 July 1941	Creation of COI
6 December 1941	Camp X (STS 103) opens in Canada
7 December 1941	Japan attacks Pearl Harbor
15 February 1942	Singapore falls to the Japanese
March 1942	Charles Jocelyn Hambro replaces Nelson as CD
13 June 1942	OSS replaces COI, placed under JCS
23 October 1942	Second battle of El Alamein
8 November 1942	Operation *Torch* – the Allied invasion of North Africa – begins
December 1942	First successful OSS infiltration into Europe (Corsica)
3 September 1943	Allies invade Italy, Italy surrenders
September 1943	Gubbins becomes director of SOE
5/6 June 1944	1st JEDBURGH teams dropped into France
6 June 1944	Operation *Overlord*, the invasion of Normandy

15 August 1944	Operation *Dragoon*, the invasion of southern France
17 September 1944	Operation *Market Garden* begins
7 May 1945	Germany surrenders
2 September 1945	Japan surrenders
20 September 1945	Executive Order 9621 abolishes the OSS
15 January 1946	SOE dissolved by Prime Minister Clement Attlee
22 January 1946	President Truman directs establishment of Central Intelligence Group, forerunner of the CIA

Prologue

Arisaig Peninsula, North-west Scotland

A lone figure stood on the edge of a forest. Looking down the hill in the direction he had to go, the bleak landscape stretched out in front of him was a daunting sight. René saw only that it led down across a stream, through a copse of trees, and then up another hill. He checked his compass again and plunged forward; no time to dawdle. The instructor had answered 'as fast as you can' when he asked how much time he had to complete the trek. He felt like he was reliving a tale out of *Boy's Own*. His rucksack chafed his shoulders and neck; his clothes, socks and boots were completely soaked; and he was hungry. He had been walking for hours, since before first light. He had been awakened earlier than usual, told to grab his gear, and with no breakfast was led down a road. An hour later, René was standing in front of his instructor, who gave him a map, a spot to find, and pushed him off on an overland trail just as dawn broke. It was the first time he had been outside on his own since he got to the manor.

Several weeks before, after being mysteriously called to an interview, René accepted an offer to try out for an interesting job. The interviewer did not precisely describe the work, but said it would engage his foreign language abilities and love of country. Faced with the option of continuing as an infantry officer, he took a chance. First there were obscure buildings and warehouses in London, where he

XX   •   NO MOON AS WITNESS

underwent several days of interviews with a few other candidates. Then he was told to take a train north to Arisaig in Scotland, where he was met on the platform by a rough-looking gentleman wearing even rougher clothing. Taken to a stately manor home, he was given some food and put to bed with explicit instructions about where he could go and what he could do on his own. The consequences of non-compliance were implicit. The days that followed were filled with classroom training on things like map reading, using a compass and survival skills. There were subjects he knew and several he didn't, like how to explain your presence in a location you weren't supposed to be. He was given a story to explain why he was at the manor, but why he would be required to use it wasn't clear. There were no morning parades or gruff sergeants to wake you up. Each man (or woman) was simply told to be somewhere at a certain time. He assumed he would be sent home if he was late. Several of René's fellow students were 'no shows', and their absence thereafter seemed to confirm his hypothesis. Walks through the terrain with the instructors reinforced the map and compass skills, but also taught things not possible in the classroom, like how to make a fire that didn't smoke. The instructors pushed them harder and faster each time they went out.

Today was different. There were no instructions, except an azimuth and distance. Then he had to look for the spot shown on the map, find a flag, go to it to get more instructions. It was a long walk and he was getting tired, but he was determined to complete the task in good time. At the edge of the stream, he loosened his rucksack straps. The water wasn't deep or very wide, but if he slipped and fell, he wanted to be able to get rid of the extra weight quickly. Without removing his sodden boots, he stepped gingerly into the freezing cold water and splashed across. On the other side, he hauled himself out and shook off as best he could before starting again. Then he looked up towards the trees in time to see two men step out of the brush. Both were in civilian clothing and carrying rifles. They waited for him. Seeing no other choice, he walked forward to

Special Forces parachutist with Halifax bomber. (Author's collection)

meet them. Before he reached them, one man, rifle butt on his hip, stepped forward and put up his hand. 'Halt,' came the command, spoken quietly but with authority. 'Who might you be and why are you here?' René stopped in his tracks; he knew the game had changed. It was day 10 and testing time had arrived.

CHAPTER 1

Origins

'In three weeks Britain will have her neck wrung like a chicken.'
                        – FRENCH GENERAL MAXIME WEYGAND, 1940

'Some chicken, some neck …'
            – WINSTON CHURCHILL, BEFORE THE HOUSE OF COMMONS,
                                    OTTAWA, 30 DECEMBER 1941

The Need Arises: SOE is Born

In the early 1930s, the embers of an unfinished war were being stirred again. German *Führer* Adolf Hitler used a mantra of Germany being stabbed in the back after World War I to set a course for a 'Thousand-Year Empire' and expand his country's power and territory, first through bluster and negotiation, then by audacity. Soon he would resort to force. Unlike the Great War of 1914–18, which seemingly began with little warning and shocked most civilians, if not their militaristic leaders, World War II was anticipated by many in the early 1930s. The rise of Hitler alarmed many from the moment the Reichstag went up in flames, taking the promise of the Weimar Republic with it. Hitler began his quest by ordering the building up of Germany's armed forces, which had been emasculated by the Treaty of Versailles following World War I. Starting in early 1935, its air force, which had been completely banned, was re-established and the Army expanded. Hitler further flouted Versailles by reoccupying the Rhineland on 7 March 1936. Two years later, on 14 March 1938, German troops marched into and annexed Austria. But Hitler was intent that still more *Lebensraum* ('living space' = territory) was needed and threatened the liberation of Germans in the Sudetenland region of Czechoslovakia, which bordered Germany. To avert war, Britain's Chamberlain and France's Daladier called for negotiations and ceded Hitler the territory he demanded without the presence or consent of the Czech government.

Chamberlain declared the Munich Agreement, signed on 30 September 1938, to be 'peace in our time', while Winston Churchill declared it 'a total and unmitigated defeat'. Churchill saw the consequences of the diplomatic surrender to Hitler as a 'first foretaste of a bitter cup'. He would be proven correct when, in March 1939, despite Hitler's assurances to the contrary, Bohemia and Moravia were subsumed as 'protectorates', while Slovakia became an ostensibly independent but servile vassal state to Germany, much like the collaborationist, aka *Pétainist*, Vichy France would later be. Britain finally began in earnest to prepare for war. Poland was obviously Hitler's next target. Britain and France reassured the Polish government of their support if Germany invaded, yet in reality, there was little they could do but watch from hundreds of miles away. Hitler had already decided Poland's fate and would invade that country on the pretext of a fake Polish attack on 1 September 1939. Three days later, Britain and France declared war on Germany, but neither ally was truly prepared to fight. Luckily, prescient men had begun to prepare for the upcoming conflict when it became apparent that Hitler would not be placated with the morsels of Austria and Czechoslovakia, and that world domination was his goal.

Foundations of the SOE

As early as 1938, a very few British senior leaders and officers began contemplating irregular warfare as another way, along with conventional military means, to counter Germany's seemingly overwhelming might. At that time, no organisation in Britain (or the United States) existed to carry out secret warfare, and the men who began to study the problem were faced with several challenges. The first was the lack of institutional knowledge; the second, a military that resisted change – especially changes that required 'ungentlemanly' conduct in warfare. Although irregular warfare has existed since human conflict began, most of its lessons had been forgotten and the concept of fighting unconventionally was never institutionalised into the conventionally minded militaries of the world. That said, there was much in recent British experience on which officers could orient themselves – not all of which was positive. The Boer War showed the British Army what a small, very mobile guerrilla force could do against a slow-moving army 10 times its size. That lesson was reinforced by the success of the British-supported Arab Revolt fought against the Ottoman-Turkish Army during World War I. That episode was followed by the 1919–21 Irish War of Independence, during which 3,000 Republican rebels confounded a force of over 75,000 British and Irish soldiers and police. There were other similar conflicts to consider: the East African campaign of German Colonel Paul Emil von Lettow-Vorbeck, whose forces never numbered more than around 15,000, kept 250,000 Commonwealth soldiers on the run for three years during World War I; while the more recent Spanish Civil War (1936–39) and the ongoing Sino-Japanese War (1937–45) demonstrated the value of unconventional warfare.

In 1936, the Deputy Chief of the Imperial General Staff (DCIGS) set up a one-man office to consider problems of tactics and organisation. Called General Staff (Research), or GS(R), it was a think-tank in which the incumbent officer could choose any topic to study and write about. In the autumn of 1938, Lieutenant Colonel J. C. F. 'Joe' Holland was assigned to the office and tasked to examine ways in which Britain might support guerrillas in Nazi-occupied Eastern Europe. He brought in two experts to help: Millis Jefferis, a Royal Engineer (RE), for his expertise in demolitions and sabotage, and Colin McVeigh Gubbins in April 1939 to study the subjects

SOE was given many code names to cover its activities, but to the public and the press it was often known by several monikers:

'Baker Street Irregulars'
'Churchill's Secret Army'
'Ministry of Ungentlemanly Warfare'

The OSS also had a few amusing nicknames:

'Oh So Secret'
'Donovan's Devils'
'Bang Bang Boys'

But one reflected its membership, a high percentage of whom were 'eastern establishment' college professors and Wall Street bankers:

'Oh So Social'

of organisation, recruitment and training. The latter was just in time for Holland's newest tasking. Having proposed and received authorisation to proceed, GS(R) began to work on three topics:

(a) To study guerilla* methods and produce a guerilla 'F.S.R.' [Field Service Regulations], incorporating detailed tactical and technical instructions, applying to each of several countries.
(b) To evolve destructive devices for delaying and suitable for use by guerillas, and capable of production and distribution on a wide enough scale to be effective.
(c) To evolve procedure and machinery for operating guerilla activities, if it should be decided to do so subsequently.

– Holland, 'General Instructions', 13 April 1939, 2, TNA: PRO, HS 8/256
(*Both Holland and Gubbins spelled 'guerrilla' with one 'r'.)

Gubbins and Jefferis took the reins for writing the 'instruction' books. Although he was an artillery officer by training, Gubbins had unique opportunities to observe unconventional warfare. Following the Great War he served on the staff of General Edmund Ironside with British forces during the Russian Civil War in 1919, before being reassigned to serve during the Irish War of Independence as brigade major to an artillery unit.

Within a short period, the two men completed three practical manuals that could be used to train resistance forces, entitled *The Partisan Leader's Handbook*, *The Art of Guerilla Warfare*, and *How to Use High Explosives*. All three were translated into several foreign languages and would be dropped to underground and guerrilla forces in Europe. They also provided the basis for the syllabus to train the operatives of SOE and OSS.

In the late summer of 1939, Gubbins departed GS(R), which had been renamed Military Intelligence (Research) or MI(R). He would soon return.

In April 1938, the director of the Secret Intelligence Service (SIS), Admiral Hugh Sinclair, tasked Major L. D. Grand, an RE officer, to study 'dirty tricks'. His small section was called 'D', for 'Destruction'. His contributions will be looked at in more detail later.

Then one more element was added to the mix. The Committee of Imperial Defence proposed the creation of the Department of Propaganda in Enemy Countries. Called simply 'Department EH', for Electra House, the building in which it was located, it was headed by Sir Campbell Stuart, who was known by his initials 'CS' in the closed circles of intelligence. EH would be plagued by chaos in its management and control until 1941.

As early as March 1939, plans for a merger of the three elements were being discussed, but this only came about after the War Cabinet put forward a proposal by the Chiefs of Staff. They suggested the formation of a secret unit to foment sabotage and subversion behind enemy lines. The proposal came out of desperation: after France had surrendered in June 1940, there was little Britain could do to counter German forces on the European continent other than small-scale actions.

Winston Churchill became Prime Minister on 10 May 1940. Having seen several sabotage operations planned by SIS go badly, he realised new thinking was necessary. He tasked the Minister of Economic Warfare (MEW), Hugh Dalton, to set up a new organisation on 22 July 1940. It was cobbled together from SIS's Section 'D', MI(R) and EH, and named the Special Operations Executive (SOE). Its mission was 'to co-ordinate all action, by way of subversion and sabotage, against the enemy overseas'.

Although not its founder, Churchill was to be SOE's most ardent supporter and protector through the war years. To make his intent clear, he told Dalton to 'set Europe ablaze'.

SOE was created out of Britain's weakness and intended to be one element of its strategic and military strategy to win the war – or at least not be defeated. Britain's other strategic priorities – bombing to cripple Germany's industrial capacity and a naval blockade to strangle its trade – would at times deprive SOE of the resources to carry out its operations.

Initially, SOE went through 'teething' problems as a number of its operations were either called off or failed outright. Although some would call the British unconventional warfare operations in Abyssinia SOE's first success, that operation – called *Mission 101* – was initially organised by MI(R) in 1940. The Abyssinian campaign would be a guidepost for SOE's future endeavours.

SOE's first successful foray into Europe would come in June 1941 with Operation *Josephine*, the sabotage of power transformers that serviced a German submarine base near Pessac in south-west France.

OSS

> 'The British were trying to push the US into war. If that be so, we were indeed a pushover.'
>
> – ERNEST CUNEO

The United States had forgotten most of its experience in irregular warfare. The US Army had its roots in fighting unconventionally against, of all people, the British. Nearly every war since that time had an unconventional aspect to it, whether fighting the Apache chieftain Vittorio or, more recently, Emilio Aguinaldo in the Philippines. Only in 1940 had the US Marine Corps even begun to consider writing a manual about 'small wars', despite its long history of engagement in police actions. The US would be starting from nearly nothing to build its special operations forces for the coming war.

From beginning to end, the driving force behind the Office of Strategic Services was William Joseph Donovan. Known as 'Wild Bill' for exploits that earned him the Medal of Honor in World War I, Donovan was a lawyer, soldier and an astute observer of political events overseas.

After his return to New York from the war in 1918, Donovan kept his eyes on the international scene. Throughout the 1920s and 1930s, he travelled far and wide to observe and report on political events and conflicts, all the while working for a New York City law firm. Witnessing events first-hand in Siberia, Manchuria and Europe convinced him the United States needed to prepare for a new type of warfare – fast-moving armoured combat supported by air assets.

One of his most controversial trips was to Ethiopia. After convincing Italian leader Benito Mussolini, *Il Duce*, that he was a private American businessman supportive of Italy, he received authorisation for a trip to observe the Italian Army's campaign to annex Ethiopia in 1935. What he saw led him to write a report that went against everything most European nations had erroneously assumed about Italy's ability to wage war. Donovan stated Italy would successfully defeat the Ethiopians despite the threat of League of Nations sanctions, and, as history would show, he was correct. Moreover, during his travels Donovan also realised that the US was handicapped by its limited intelligence collection and analysis capabilities.

As World War II approached, the US Army's under-manned and under-funded Military Intelligence Division (MID) and the Navy's Office of Naval Intelligence (ONI) were restricted, for the most part, to collecting overt (open source) military information. The Department of State conducted analysis of political intelligence but did no operational intelligence work. Finally, there was J. Edgar Hoover's Federal Bureau of Investigation (FBI), which was charged with investigating espionage, counter-espionage and sabotage. There was no authority to centralise and coordinate intelligence operations in the United States.

In 1940, the war in Europe was well underway, with Britain the only undefeated survivor – its troops having been withdrawn from the continent through a hastily improvised, but brilliantly executed evacuation at Dunkirk. Russia was still Germany's ally, and would remain so until attacked in June 1941. Much of France was occupied by Germany, with the remainder under the thumb of the collaborationist Vichy regime.

In June 1940, US President Franklin Delano Roosevelt (FDR) wanted a survey carried out of Britain's defence capabilities and 'Fifth Column' activities in Europe, an idea made at the suggestion of Frank Knox, Secretary of the Navy. It was Knox who did most of the initial coordination. He asked two men to go to Britain: Edgar Mowrer, a *Chicago Daily News* correspondent, and William Donovan, a close friend and fellow Republican. On their return, Donovan and Mowrer would co-author a public-awareness pamphlet warning of the dangers of German covert propaganda called *Fifth Column Lessons for America*.

Secretary Knox informed the British Ambassador to the United States, Lord Lothian, of the impending visit, and it was through the letters of both men that Donovan was given full access to British war preparations.

It was at this moment that William S. Stephenson came onto the scene. Stephenson was the chief of British Security Coordination (BSC), a cover office for the SIS in New York – his cover title was Passport Control Officer (PCO). Winston Churchill had tasked him to establish liaison between SIS and the FBI, and, most importantly, to persuade the United States to supply Britain with much-needed war materials which were embargoed because of neutrality laws. Stephenson had already met with J. Edgar Hoover in early 1940, an event orchestrated by Ernst Cuneo, an influential lawyer and friend of FDR. The result of those meetings was the establishment of an information exchange that facilitated counter-espionage efforts in the Western Hemisphere. Although Stephenson's work in the US was keyed on countering Nazi propaganda and setting up intelligence liaison, his intercession was also instrumental in the formulation of the Lend-Lease Agreement that provided Britain much-needed war materials in exchange for long-term leases for US bases on Commonwealth territory.

Stephenson learned of Donovan's summer 1940 trip to London. He sent word to London to arrange a meeting with the man known as 'C', SIS Director Stuart Menzies, to discuss German propaganda efforts. Donovan met not only with British military and political leaders, but with Prime Minister Winston Churchill. Gathering as much information as possible, he returned to Washington to brief Knox and others and to reassure them that Britain was prepared to resist any invasion.

Donovan made a second, longer visit across the Atlantic a few months later. According to Donovan, the president had requested he make yet another appreciation visit to England and also the Mediterranean. This he did. From December 1940 to February 1941 he undertook an exhaustive journey to see as much as possible, which the British fully supported, now realising his value to their cause. Stephenson would travel with 'Wild Bill' this time and assist him to delve deeper into the murky world of British intelligence and special operations, including meeting with Sir Frank Nelson, then head of the new SOE, and the War Cabinet and Joint Chiefs of Staff, as well as the Ministry of Economic Warfare.

Donovan came home with a head full of ideas on how America could contribute to the war. Most importantly, he also had a general sketch of how the US should organise its efforts in the areas of propaganda, intelligence and sabotage. Stephenson, seeing

Designating a Coordinator of Information

By virtue of the authority vested in me as President of the United States and as Commander in Chief of the Army and Navy of the United States, it is ordered as follows:

1. There is hereby established the position of Coordinator of Information, with authority to collect and analyze all information and data, which may bear upon national security; to correlate such information and dates and to make such information and data available to the President and to such departments and officials of the Government as the President may determine; and to carry out, when requested by the President, such supplementary activities as may facilitate the securing of information important for national security not now available to the Government.

2. The several departments and agencies of the Government shall make available to the Coordinator of Information all and any such information and data relating to national security as the Coordinators with the approval of the President may from time to time request.

3. The Coordinator of Information may appoint such committees, consisting of appropriate representatives of the various departments and agencies of the Government, as he may deem necessary to assist him in the performance of his functions.

4. Nothing in the duties and responsibilities of the Coordinator of Information shall in any way interfere with or impair the duties and responsibilities of the regular military and naval advisers of the President as Commander in Chief of the Army and Navy.

5. Within the limits of such funds as may be allocated to the Coordinator of Information by the President, the

> Coordinator may employ necessary personnel and make provision for the necessary supplies, facilities, and services.
> 6. William J. Donovan is hereby designated as Coordinator of Information.
>
> Franklin D. Roosevelt
> The White House,
> July 11, 1941

a candidate for even closer cooperation than Hoover, was quite willing to amplify and direct Donovan's thinking.

The US Government was still plagued by a lack of information sharing and intelligence coordination between its various civilian and military agencies. FDR asked three cabinet officials – Secretary of War Henry Stimson, Attorney General Robert Jackson and Secretary of the Navy Frank Knox – to form a committee to look at the problem. Jackson had oversight of Hoover's FBI and Knox was, of course, Donovan's friend. Called upon to give his advice, Donovan wrote a proposal that advocated the creation of a centralised intelligence agency that would be responsible for both propaganda and subversion. It was based on the British model Donovan had observed during his travels

The committee concurred with Donovan's ideas and sent them forward to FDR, who then asked Donovan to come up with a specific plan. He did and presented it to FDR with what he called a 'Memorandum of Establishment of Service of Strategic Information' on 10 June 1941.

FDR accepted Donovan's plan and issued a 'military order' establishing the COI (Coordinator of Information). It was officially founded on 11 July 1941.

In October 1941, FDR informed Winston Churchill of the action and that Donovan would be sending a small staff to London.

The fact that the COI had been established under FDR's direct supervision rankled the Joint Chiefs of Staff (JCS) and Hoover to no end. J. Edgar jealously guarded his bureau's turf and wanted no encroachment from any other organisation into his realm. COI and the later OSS would be restricted from conducting operations in the Western Hemisphere, which was allocated to the FBI. The JCS, or more precisely, the MID and ONI, were concerned that Donovan's organisation would duplicate their work. Donovan, along with Brigadier General Walter B. Smith, found a way around this by naming COI an 'agency of the JCS' in March 1942, effectively subordinating it to the military chiefs although it was not a 'military' organisation.

One final adjustment was made to Donovan's plan when FDR directed that the COI's Foreign Information Service, which broadcast 'white' propaganda, be moved to the Office of War Information. COI would keep its 'black' propaganda effort. With those changes to its organisation, the COI became the Office of Strategic Services (OSS) on 13 June 1942.

Donovan's thinking on how his organisation would approach the looming war can be discerned in a memo he wrote to FDR on 22 December 1941:

> On the offensive, this kind of operation is necessary in order to disintegrate the resistance. On the defensive, it is necessary in order to harass the enemy as local conditions may permit.
>
> We can consider this under two types of guerrilla warfare:
>
> 1. Setting up of small groups working as bands under definite leaders.
> 2. The establishment of guerrilla forces, military in nature, in order to secure cohesion and successfully carry out a plan of campaign.
>
> It is unnecessary to stress that modern large-sized armies are greatly dependent on roads, railways, and signal communications, and the creation of supply and munitions dumps, to keep themselves supplied with food, munitions and gasoline – without which they cannot operate. These communications constitute a desirable target both of the military and sabotage type.

The principle laid down is that the whole art of guerrilla warfare lies in striking the enemy where he least expects it and yet where he is most vulnerable.

Specifically, I suggest the following:

1. That as an essential part of any strategic plan, there be recognized the need of sewing (sic) the dragon's teeth in those territories from which we must withdraw and in which the enemy will place his army; for example, the Azores or North Africa. That the aid of native chiefs be obtained, the loyalty of the inhabitants be cultivated; Fifth columnists organized and placed, demolition material cached; and guerrilla bands of bold and daring men organized and installed.
2. That there be organized now, in the United States, a guerrilla corps independent and separate from the Army and Navy, and imbued with a maximum of the offensive and imaginative spirit. This force should, of course, be created along disciplined military lines, analogous to the British Commando principle, a statement of which I sent you recently.

The OSS's first deployments took place in January 1942 when around a dozen officers were sent under the cover of 'Vice-Consuls' to Tangiers, where they collected intelligence and prepared the way for the Operation *Torch* landings in North Africa in November that year.

Organisation and Control

SOE

Although the SOE was set up under Hugh Dalton's Ministry of Economic Warfare (MEW), it was remarkably independent of ministerial oversight. Dalton served as SOE's strong arm with Whitehall where necessary, but its day-to-day operations were very much hidden from the scrutiny of the public and, more importantly, parliament. Dalton chose Sir Frank Nelson to be SOE's first director. Nelson would keep Dalton briefed on the intricacies of SOE's operations. He would be known by the signature he used on his papers: 'CD'.

At that time, there was little to brief on, as unconventional operations were slow to organise with a still fledgling resistance across most of Europe. Where there were possibilities, like Poland, the distances were just too far for the available means to project forces or operatives.

In early 1942, Dalton left MEW to be replaced by Lord Selborne, who quickly saw that Nelson had exceeded his 'best by' date; he was simply burnt out. Selborne brought in Sir Charles Hambro to take his place. Despite his combat experiences in Scandinavia, for which he was knighted, Hambro fell out with Selborne from the beginning. His useful life in SOE began to ebb with his insistence that SOE operations remain independent from military control. Taking such a view ensured secrecy but also meant that theatre commanders had no idea what SOE could do for them. Because of that, SOE could not get the assistance it required. The final straw came when Hambro decided to withhold information about a particular incident from his boss. When Selborne was caught uninformed about that event by his peers and the Prime Minister, he summarily told Hambro he must leave.

Colin Gubbins returned in November 1940 as SOE's Director of Training and Operations and was next in line for the directorship. As it turned out, he was an inspired choice. For one, he was an army officer and understood the necessity of coordinating with and supporting the military commander. Second, he was an inspiring leader.

Early in the war, SOE was directed to prepare a two-phase plan to support an Allied invasion of Europe – the eventual end game when conventional forces could attack and defeat Germany. They were to do this by first reducing the fighting strength of the enemy by any means, fraying the edges of the Axis in faraway places like Africa and the Balkans, while building up intelligence and sabotage networks on the continent. Second, they would help train resistance forces and build up secret armies to carry out actions that would lower the enemy's morale, and raise revolts that would destabilise the occupied territories and disrupt the enemy's rear areas. These two aims constituted SOE's short- and long-range strategic planning.

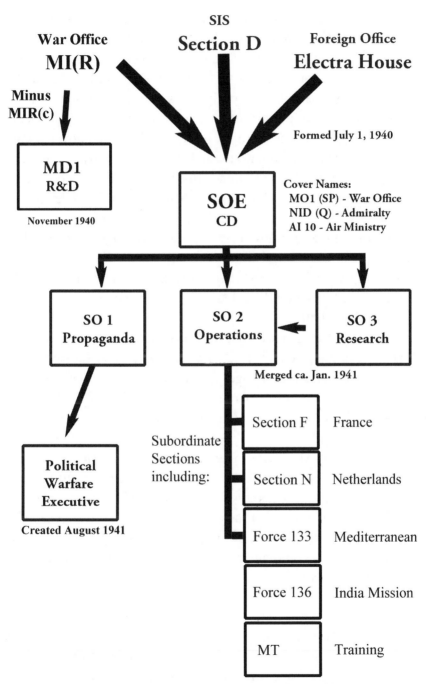

SOE organisation showing selected branches and offices.

SOE's operations were generally conceived and planned in a straightforward methodology. The SOE 'Board of Directors' and the Joint Planning Staff (JPS) would agree on general policies that would result in operational directives being issued. These would act as blueprints for operational planning. In some cases, policy planning was accomplished in collaboration with the governments-in-exile of the respective target country. In others, the exiled governments were not consulted, which often led to complaints from them and protests from the Foreign Office. This would lead to a policy later described by M. R. D. Foot as 'No bangs without Foreign Office approval'.

The 'Board' was composed of SOE's senior department and section officers, who were both military and civilians and were all subject matter experts in their respective fields. This brain trust devised the policies and translated them into projects that could be carried out by operations staff.

As originally organised, SOE was made up of three departments. There was Propaganda (SO1), Operations (SO2) and Research (SO3), but as ever in wartime, changes happened rapidly. SO3 was merged into SO2, and SO1 was separated off to form the Political Warfare Executive (PWE) after the Ministry of Information challenged its mission. (See p.15)

There were also research and development departments that were responsible for acquiring or devising special equipment to meet current operational needs as well as anticipated future requirements.

All in all, SOE was very much an organisation in flux. It was, after all, new and attempting to accomplish something unprecedented. As we will see, while many of its operations went well, some went spectacularly wrong.

OSS

The OSS followed the SOE in many areas, but because it had a few more missions, its organisation was more complex. Not only was it tasked with special operations – sabotage, subversion and guerrilla warfare – it also conducted secret intelligence collection operations, which in Britain was the responsibility of SIS. Donovan's decision to incorporate both the intelligence and military functions into one organisation was based on the recommendations of Robert Solborg. Donovan sent Solborg to London to observe SOE. There he saw how the turf battles between SOE and SIS hampered operations. A pointed comment by SOE officer Christopher 'Monty' Woodhouse illustrates the tension between the two organisations: 'SOE was a completely different bureau than SIS. All those who consider SOE officers as agents of the SIS as well, delude themselves.' Donovan was determined to avoid that problem.

With his appointment as Coordinator of Strategic Information on 11 July 1941, Donovan quickly began to assemble the personnel his new organisation would need. With war came a new urgency and changes to the COI. In June 1942, it was reorganised and renamed the Office of Strategic Services. Although it had lost its mandate to conduct counter-intelligence operations in Latin and South America to J. Edgar Hoover's FBI, as well as its propaganda branch (but not psychological warfare) to the Office of War Information, the OSS would see its other missions of unconventional warfare and espionage expanded.

Donovan's OSS was placed under the newly formed Joint Chiefs of Staff and given its support and aegis, although he still reported to the President. OSS's relationship with JCS was not always smooth – the Navy and Army had serious reservations about giving a 'civilian' agency any responsibility for intelligence operations. In the end, a compromise was achieved and the OSS was able to grow and operate as the United States' premier agency for intelligence and unconventional warfare without interference (if not grumbling) from the military.

Donovan served as OSS director until the organisation was disbanded in 1946. Assisting him in the role was the OSS Planning Group, which was made up of four military officers – two each from the Army and Navy – four OSS officers, one State Department officer

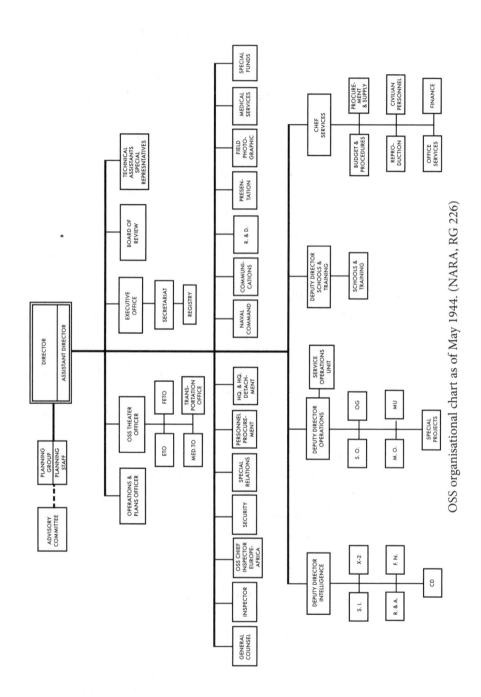

OSS organisational chart as of May 1944. (NARA, RG 226)

The Maritime Unit developed equipment that included a folding, two-man kayak, called a Klepper, that was also adopted by SOE and the British Special Boat Section (SBS), as well as an underwater breathing apparatus. Christian J. Lambertsen developed an Amphibious Respiratory Unit, a rebreather or closed-circuit device that did not produce tell-tale bubbles. His rig was the first to be known by the acronym 'SCUBA', for self-contained underwater breathing apparatus, and his work led to the formation of the MU's 'Operational Swimmer Group'.

and an Advisory Committee, that brought in specialists from other bureaus and departments as required.

All major OSS projects and plans were first discussed in the Planning Group and, after approval by the director (Donovan), submitted to the JCS for final approval.

Importantly, from the beginning all OSS officers and operatives in the field were under the direct control of the theatre commander through an OSS liaison officer. The theatre commander had final approval authority over any operation before it was launched and was kept informed of all operations before, during and after their initiation.

Between 1941 and 1944, the organisation underwent several changes. Donovan had three deputies who controlled the major branches, with a number of smaller offices attending to specialised duties like recruitment, research and development, or photography.

First, there was the Deputy Director for Schools and Training (DST). Obviously, this branch was responsible for basic and advanced training of personnel. Recruitment was handled by a separate section for security reasons.

The Deputy Director of Operations (DDO), the second major branch, controlled the following:

- Special Operations (SO) Branch, whose mission was the planning and coordination of sabotage, guerrilla warfare, and support and supply of resistance groups.
- Operational Groups (OG) that organised and trained small teams to operate behind enemy lines as nuclei for guerrilla warfare units.
- Morale Operations (MO) Branch, which was responsible for the conduct of subversion other than physical, including 'black' propaganda.
- Maritime Unit (MU), originally under SO, which conducted infiltration of operatives or agents for other branches by sea; supply of resistance groups and others by sea; execution of maritime sabotage; and the development of special equipment and devices for maritime ops.
- Special Projects Office (SPO), which had responsibility for developing weapons of sabotage and securing intelligence on enemy secret weapons.

The third major branch was the Deputy Director of Intelligence (DDI) that controlled:

- Secret Intelligence (SI) Branch, whose missions included espionage and counter-espionage in enemy-occupied or controlled territories. Bases were allowed to be established in neutral countries best suited for the purpose. It was also charged with maintaining contact with underground groups in enemy-occupied or controlled territory.
- Research and Analysis Branch, which was one of the most respected sections of OSS because of the high quality and expansive nature of its analysis, not only of the enemy's military, but political and economic issues that affected the Axis powers and its occupied territories. It had three major tasks:
  1) collection, compilation and analysis of such political, psychological warfare, sociological and economic

information and its preparation in such form as may be required for military operations.

2)   assembling from all available sources of documentary and pictorial data required in the preparation of studies requested by authorised agencies.

3)   preparation of such maps, charts, illustrations and visual presentations as were required by the JCS and the War and Navy Departments.

Before operations could be launched, however, it was necessary to recruit, train, equip and prepare the operatives of SOE and OSS for deployment. It should be noted that the methods both organisations used have stood the test of time and are used today, with minor adjustments, to assess and select the special operators of both Britain and the US.

CHAPTER 2

Assessment, Selection and Training

Both the SOE and OSS began with virtually blank slates to guide how they were to build and man their organisation. The unconventional exploits of the Boer War, World War I and thereafter had largely been forgotten by both countries' militaries. Those few men who did remember would use their experience to build new unconventional warfare forces to face off against the Axis enemy.

As described earlier, Britain began preparing and training for unconventional warfare in 1938, while its first operations took place in 1940. With their later entry into the war, the Americans would benefit from British experiences.

In November 1940, SOE profited from the return of Colin Gubbins as Director of Training and Operations. After leaving SOE, he spent nearly the first year of World War II serving with the Military Mission to Poland and then leading the Independent Companies in Norway (the first Commandos). Once again under the command of General Ironside, Gubbins was tasked to organise the short-term protection of Britain by setting up the 'Auxiliary Units', essentially a home defence force organised to harass and harry a German invasion. He was now even more experienced to take on the mission of training SOE's operatives.

The first puzzle was where to find the men and women to do the work. That was just one of several difficult questions faced by the organisations. As both were secret, they could not advertise to fill their positions. Furthermore, with no unconventional warfare experts to choose from, how could one recruit? The leadership of SOE and OSS fell back on an old standby: recruit people you know and trust, then train them to accomplish the mission.

While this worked to a large extent, there were failures, as some recruits were trusted but their true loyalties were never fully verified. Kim Philby, who taught SOE operatives in the darker arts of propaganda at Beaulieu and later defected to the Soviet Union, was one such oversight. Duncan Lee, an executive assistant to William Donovan and a communist, was another. Both were recruited agents of the Soviet NKVD. While SIS was adamant about not employing staff officers who had previous affiliations with communists or fascists, SOE, and later OSS, sometimes bent the rules in that regard. In the field, recruitment of anyone who could assist to bring down the Nazi regime was the rule, until the Foreign Office complained.

The recruitment process changed during the course of the war as manpower needs increased and the requirements of clandestine intelligence and special operations became better understood. Although their methods were initially similar, the British and American assessment and selection (A&S) process differed more widely as the war progressed and OSS matured.

The British Method

The recruitment process for the operatives destined for possible deployment to France (F Section) described in M. R. D. Foot's officially sanctioned history of the SOE illustrates the early methodology used. The procedure for each geographical section generally followed this format.

Initially, a prospective operative (sometimes called an 'agent', but never a 'spy') was interviewed in obscure locations around London to determine his or her language capability and suitability for operations. Starting out in English, the interviewer would quickly shift to French, expecting the candidate to be completely comfortable in the target country's language. If they weren't, the interview ended. If they were, the questions would continue to determine the person's knowledge of France and the regions they knew well or in which they were known by others.

Slowly, over the course of several encounters on separate days, the interviewer would peel back the layers of the onion. The interviewer was specifically chosen for his ability to read people – not just what they said, but how they said it (or didn't), gave him clues as to their motivations and suitability for service. Obviously, intelligence, as well as the appropriate motivation, i.e. not pathological hatred, were desired. The ability to make rational decisions under stress was paramount. Any display of rashness, overconfidence or inability to keep a secret was a disqualifying factor. SOE was looking for chess players, not aggressive gamblers.

At the same time, the candidate would be given subtle clues as to the nature of the work he or she would be asked to perform to determine their willingness to risk their life. At the final meeting, the now prospective operatives would be offered the opportunity to try out for a special mission, but also be told their chances of getting killed were about equal to returning home. When the war was over, it turned out the risk had been overplayed a bit: around 25 per cent or one in four operatives would not return. Those odds were about the same as serving with the German submarine service, but certainly better than being a junior officer in World War I. The candidate would be given several days to think about it – no quick decisions were accepted – and were then sent to training.

Those selected went on to a two- to three-week preliminary course at one of several country houses on estates outside London. There they would be subjected to intense physical fitness, map-reading and basic firearms training. These were the same sort of skills taught to a soldier in basic training, except these participants were more rigorously scrutinised. This course served as a second filter to separate the wheat from the chaff. The classes became smaller by the day. At any point in the training, student operatives who failed, quit or were simply assessed as unsuitable were sent to the 'cooler' at Inverlair, Scotland, where they were isolated until it was decided they couldn't or wouldn't endanger ongoing operations.

In 1943, the process was altered to incorporate lessons learned and accommodate the increased flow of candidates needed for operations. A Students' Assessment Board (SAB) was set up that exchanged the individual interview for a battery of interviews and tests conducted by psychologists who were thoroughly familiar with the requirements needed for SOE's activities. Among these were an ability to work with, organise and train resistance groups, to collect intelligence, act as radio operators or sabotage enemy targets. Many other skills were needed for service in the field and on the home front, including administrators, planners, security and support personnel, research and development, propaganda specialists and cryptographers. All these roles needed reliable, skilled and trustworthy people to fill the jobs.

The SAB operated out of Special Training School (STS) 7 at Cranleigh in Surrey, where the 'students' would be subjected to a four-day battery of tests to reliably predict their usefulness to the organisation. Note that the tests results are caveated as 'reliably predict' because no test can be 100 per cent conclusive as to how someone will behave under the pressures of clandestine or covert operations. What the tests were intended to do was eliminate unfit candidates; those who would probably fail training, not be able to perform their duties properly or imperil the security of the organisation. The new process was quicker and better at assessing the students at a time when special skills were in high demand.

Those who survived the first cuts went on to the Paramilitary Course, a four-week, deeper indoctrination in military skills, much of which had been developed by MI(R) officer Major F. T. Davies before he joined SOE. 'Tommy' Davies was rare because he had actual experience fighting clandestinely against the Germans, having spirited away and destroyed bearer bonds worth millions in the Netherlands before the enemy could get their hands on the negotiable instruments. Davies put together the original four-part training plan, which remained more or less intact for the entire life of SOE. It included the Preliminary, Paramilitary and Finishing Schools, prior to the final pre-mission briefing segment at what were called the Holding Schools.

The paramilitary segment included subjects that had been taught in the Preliminary School but at a much more intense and detailed level. No longer was the instruction solely a method of assessment; the skills taught were to be mastered as if the operatives' lives depended on them, which they would. Weapons training was more detailed and involved not only firing the commonly issued SOE weapons such as the Sten and Thompson sub-machine guns, but also enemy weapons that might be encountered in the operative's area of operations.

Along with weapons skills, unarmed combat was taught by specialists in the field. Two of the most famous were Eric A. Sykes and William E. Fairbairn, both of whom had served with the Shanghai Municipal Police. Fairbairn, known as 'Dangerous Dan', and Sykes were exceptionally gifted unarmed combat (combative), pistol and knife fighting instructors. They were also the designers of the eponymous 'Fairbairn-Sykes' commando knife. Fairbairn lived by the credo that in a street fight or in combat there was 'no fair play, no rules except one: *kill or be killed*'. Sykes was a bit more moderate in his views but still ended every demonstration with the exhortation, 'and then, kick him in the testicles'. A third instructor, lesser known today but just as formidable, was Colonel Leonard Hector Grant-Taylor.

More detailed training in cross-country navigation, survival, first aid, demolitions and sabotage was given while students continued to be evaluated not only for suitability, but whether they had special talents that might be used in a particular niche. Specialist schools would further refine a student's abilities by teaching advanced demolitions and sabotage, micro-photography, lock picking and radio operations. Throughout the training programme, emphasis

A quote from a later Special Air Service (SAS) guide on close-quarter battle is worth repeating because it encapsulates the purpose of the training:

> The aim of CQB training is to guarantee success in killing. It is much more of a personal affair than ordinary combat and it is just not good enough to temporarily put your opponent out of action so that he can live to fight another day. He must be definitely and quickly killed so that you can switch your whole attention onto the next target. Besides obvious physical abilities, the CQB operator must be cool-headed and, above all, remorseless. The end product of CQB training must be automatic and instantaneous killing.

was placed not on training a soldier who was effective under close leadership, but on the development of 'individual initiative, personal courage and resourcefulness'.

One of the most important specialist schools was STS 17, located at Brickendonbury Manor near Hertford. Here students learned the finer points of industrial sabotage from experts like Lieutenant Colonel George Rheam, whom M. R. D. Foot regards as the 'founder' of the art. Students visited factories to understand their weak points, and had access to trains and airplanes so they could learn how to quickly destroy or cripple them with a minimum of explosives or even by removing essential parts.

Paramilitary training was given at STS 21 through to 25c in the Arisaig and Morar areas of Scotland. When the Germans, who never had a great sense of humour, found out about the network of schools they called it the 'International Gangster School'.

When SOE began training other nationalities, they would be kept together and trained at one site. Czech operatives, for example, trained at STS 25, while the Norwegians trained at STS 26 – Drumintoul Lodge in the Cairngorms. Once paramilitary training was completed, the students received five days of parachute training at STS 51 located at Ringway Airfield near Manchester.

Parachute-qualified Americans even had to take part because SOE's and OSS's specialised aircraft had unusual exits called 'Joe Holes', which required parachutists undergo additional training.

Final training was undertaken at the 'Finishing Schools' around Beaulieu in the New Forest. It was only here that the students finally learned the true purpose of their training and their true employer: the SOE. Many had guessed already, but had not been specifically told prior to reaching this stage.

The final training course was physically easier compared to the paramilitary section, but no less arduous mentally. Here the operatives learned the subtle arts of intelligence tradecraft – how to communicate secretly, conduct surveillance and counter-surveillance, or react to questioning at a control point or by security personnel on the streets. Exercises showed them how to resist more determined interrogation should they be arrested. More detailed instruction in propaganda, cryptography and communications was also provided. Although specialist schools taught designated operatives the technical aspects of radios used to maintain contact with headquarters, all operatives were expected to know the basics of Morse code and how to encrypt and send messages properly and securely.

In the end, it was hoped that careful screening and the intensive training had produced an operative who had the conspiratorial behavioural skills and demeanour to survive as part of an underground in the city, as well as in the field. Determination, adaptability, flexibility and innovation were equally important for the individual operator. The operatives needed to have the stamina to work for long periods on their own in difficult and hazardous environments. Soon, the operatives would rely on their wits, training, language skills and cover identities to protect them.

With the final training hurdle out of the way, fully vetted and trained operatives moved to the Holding Schools which served as the final way station for mission and security briefings, issuance of documentation, clothing and equipment before they were dispatched to their operational area. For some the wait would be weeks or months; for others merely days would pass before they jumped into danger.

> 'By the end of the war, SOE schools had trained 6,810 students, of whom only 480 were full-fledged British SOE operatives; the rest were from sixteen foreign nations, as well as 872 students from the Secret Intelligence Service and 172 from the Special Air Service.'
>
> – Major G. M. Forty, 'History of the Training Section of SOE, 1940–1945', 206, TNA: PRO, HS 7/51

The American Method

When setting up their new organisation, the OSS benefited greatly from SOE's experience, even though the United States had not been idle. Colonel Donovan's overseas trips to observe British readiness had served him well. On his first visit in July 1940, he was introduced to SIS and SOE operations and training methods. The visit served to inform and reinforce Donovan's ideas on how to organise and train what would become OSS. His second trip gave him a close and intimate view of SOE's training, organisation and operations in the Mediterranean and the Balkans. 'Wild Bill' decided, appropriately enough, that his operatives should be 'Ph.D.s who could win a bar fight'.

In early 1941, as Donovan began to select the core members of what would become the OSS leadership team, he decided the first step was to determine how to approach and train for the mission. He tasked the senior leaders to study what the unit would be tasked with: clandestine intelligence collection and special operations. While the staff of the fledgling unit was planning, the organisation was not yet moving ahead with anything other than the most basic recruitment. In the autumn of 1941, training had not begun. That was about to suddenly change.

An important development took place at a September 1941 meeting at BSC chief Stephenson's flat in New York. The conversations there led to the construction of a SOE training facility on Lake Ontario in Canada called Camp X. In the SOE facilities roster, it was known as STS 103 and replicated facilities in Britain, albeit all in one 275-acre location. Donovan, who had input into the project, did not want to send operatives off to grand country homes for training. STS 103 was used to train prospective operatives from Canada and other Commonwealth countries, but from the beginning it was set up in anticipation of the Americans entering the war. It opened on 6 December 1941, the day before Japan attacked Pearl Harbor.

The first group of Americans arrived at the camp in February of the following year for a four-week training course. Among the students was Major Garland Williams, who, along with around 12 others, would make up OSS's instructor cadre. The first students from SO Branch would arrive in April. Camp X not only trained operatives, but 'harmonised' SOE and OSS operations from the very beginning.

Prospective OSS operatives were initially recruited haphazardly without any type of uniform screening. Many thus recruited were simply unfit for the job. In late 1943, OSS developed a three-day programme to select candidates who would be suited to the unconventional mission that awaited them. It was administered by psychiatrists and psychologists who developed a programme based on examples used by the German and British militaries. The tests were administered at an input site called 'Station S' and, when the flow became too great, a second site in Washington, known cleverly enough as 'Station W'. When more operatives were needed for the Asia-Pacific theatre, a third assessment facility, 'Station WS', was established at San Clemente, California.

The difficulties involved in setting up the assessment and selection process were myriad. One of the most difficult was assessing individuals for what were essentially unique jobs with requirements that were largely unknown. This led to a decision to judge each candidate on general qualifications that were applicable to the great majority of OSS assignments. These methods are well described in the unclassified OSS study *Assessment of men; selection of personnel for the Office of Strategic Services.*

In the assessment phase, candidates were stripped of all symbols of rank and their individual persona laid bare; they were given a pseudonym and made to wear army fatigues without insignia of any kind. This not only dispossessed the candidate, but stripped them of any preconceived notions of rank, superiority or inferiority. In other words, it levelled the playing field.

Candidates were evaluated on seven major variables: 1) motivation; 2) energy and initiative; 3) effective intelligence; 4) emotional stability; 5) social relations; 6) leadership; and 7) security. Additionally, three other qualifications were assessed: 8) physical ability; 9) observing and reporting; and 10) propaganda skills.

Along with straightforward physical tests, such as an obstacle course, diverse written and field tests revealed each candidate's personal attributes. The candidates were tested on their ability to remember details of a map. Leadership was measured by having them build a bridge across a stream, with two assistants who made the experience as difficult as possible. Another test required the candidate to write a short intelligence report based on several 'captured' documents. Often there was no correct solution to the test; the objective was to observe and evaluate each candidate's performance.

A prospective operative's resourcefulness was tested using a stressful interrogation scenario. The subject was given 12 minutes to devise a cover story to explain his presence in a building and then subjected to intense questioning. In all cases, the story would fall apart at some point, but one of the more notable reactions was by a man who had been arrested by the Gestapo before the war. When subjected to the test interrogation, he was so unnerved by the experience that he quit the programme.

The most crucial piece of the puzzle was an interview that was administered after all other data on a candidate was assembled. Conducted by a psychologist, it followed no strict form, but was meant to allow the candidate to reveal as much about him or herself as possible and permit an accurate prediction of future performance.

As with the British system, there were no perfect answers, but the assessment programme improved the chances of matching the correct person to the mission.

These tests, along with the initial recruitment evaluation, served as the basis for decisions about who went on to the core training course at Camp X or sites within the United States. The Canadian camp continued its operations through the duration of the war, but Donovan also set up training areas in the United States, most of them ringed around the Washington DC area.

Initially, there were two distinct curricula: one was designed to prepare operatives for espionage; the second to prepare personnel for various forms of sabotage and the training of guerrilla units. These would be merged when it was realised that the tradecraft involved in clandestine operations, both for espionage and sabotage, were basically the same. Specialised training would be provided separately after the basic course was completed.

Training days at the camps ran much like those in England and Scotland, with intense physical exercise followed by lectures or training with weapons and explosives. The Camp X instructors were of the same calibre as those in Britain. In fact, some were actually the same – William Fairbairn was sent to Canada to assist with the setting up of training while Sykes was left behind to continue the programme in Britain.

Fairbairn set up a marksmanship facility that mirrored those of Scotland, the most notorious of which was his 'House of Horrors'. The shooting house was built to simulate conditions an operative would encounter inside a building, such as moving in tight spaces, encountering hostile and friendly targets suddenly at short range. This put pressure on the shooter that could not be replicated on the standard range. Darkness and smoke could be used to limit visibility and bring even more realism into the equation.

Trainees would not be given notice before they were subjected to a scenario. They would be awoken at night, given a pistol with loaded magazines and shown the entrance. Their instructions were to shoot any enemy guards they encountered. Accompanied by an instructor, the shooter would make his or her way through a maze-like corridor with uneven flooring to throw them off balance, and be confronted by targets that were controlled by wires and springs. It tested the operative's weapons handling and target discrimination, as well as their coolness under pressure.

At other training sites, the operatives would also be required to negotiate rope bridges over cold mountain streams or obstacle courses that tested strength, balance and nerve, as well as leadership.

The students' capabilities would be revealed and evaluated through exercises that might include a parachute drop into an unknown landing zone and long march back to camp, or the penetration of a simulated enemy factory for a sabotage mission. The conclusion of the course meant the graduates were ready for the real test: that of facing the enemy on his own turf.

Once the operatives finished training they could count on two things. For most, the first would be a lot of waiting and false starts before they got the 'two eggs' on their breakfast plate that indicated they were to parachute into their target country that night. The second was the knowledge that they would be on their own in enemy territory. Terror and boredom have always been two hallmarks of intelligence and military operations – but in the case of SOE and OSS operatives it was the pervasive feeling of being surrounded by the enemy. Fear, in varying degrees, was omnipresent.

As members of a team, whether a three-man JEDBURGH or a 20-man Operational Group, there was some comfort in numbers. While that did not guarantee safety, at least there were others who would share the danger and provide mutual cover.

For the individual operative there was much to be concerned with. Unless they had previous experience at this sort of subterfuge (as did many of the criminals and communists), or were accomplished 'con'-artists or just natural actors, there was always the fear of discovery when they presented their documents for the first time. While the quality of their papers might be impeccable, there was always a chance that a change had been made or a new requirement instituted that was not yet known to the forgers in England. Would their story hold up, their language skills be enough, or would a simple nervous tic arouse suspicions?

For the radio operator who might not speak the local language well, there were many hours each day of tedium or loneliness waiting in a safe house for that hour of high anxiety when they came up on the air to transmit. Had they regularly changed their radio's location? Would the direction-finding (DF) teams lock on to their signal, and would the police or Gestapo be able to triangulate their position in time to find and arrest them? A pistol might be close at hand, but would it help them escape arrest or commit suicide?

There are stories, probably enhanced by the instructors at Beaulieu, of an operative who used the wrong hand to eat his steak or looked the wrong way before crossing a street and was arrested. Whether true or not, the tales served to underline the necessity to be constantly aware of your surroundings and who might be listening or watching. Many could operate under this stress without a care, while others lived in constant terror of discovery.

Whether it was patriotism, a search for adventure, a desire for revenge or a simple wish to be their own master when the alternative was to be a soldier at the front, each operative was motivated to serve their country in one of the most dangerous of endeavours.

Many singleton operatives would experience close encounters with the enemy security forces. Most usually passed scrutiny without a problem. Some were arrested but escaped or managed to convince their interrogators of their innocence. Some managed to shoot their way out or run away to survive another day. Others, about one in four, did not.

OSS Scope of Training

SO agents and operatives are selected for their intelligence, courage, and natural resourcefulness in dealing with resistance groups. In addition they must have stamina to be able to live and move about undetected in their area of operation. Normally, they should be fluent in the local language and be a native of a nationality acceptable to the authorities and people of the area.

Basic training courses are provided by the Schools and Training Branch. The Special Operations Branch collaborates with that Branch by developing satisfactory training courses for the schools. Training is a continuous process and it is the responsibility of each SO chief, both in the United States and in the field to see that training progresses satisfactorily.

Because of the hazardous nature and specialized technical requirements of SO, it is important that every individual in the organization receive a thorough schooling in the work he has to perform. For field operatives and all those having to do with planning, servicing, and commanding field operatives, training starts with the basic school courses which include instruction in secret intelligence and morale operations as well as special operations. Special schooling for each mission is given to the individuals assigned to it. For specific tasks schooling becomes intensive and detailed and concludes in a final briefing or instruction just prior to the execution of the mission.

The SO operative must be able to assume perfect cover or concealment. He must know how to employ underground methods of communication without undue risk to himself or others. He must know how to recruit, incite, train, and direct the operations of agents, saboteurs, resistance groups, and agents provocateur.

The saboteur, according to the methods he is to employ, should be skilled in sabotage by resistance, or by destruction, or against personnel, or by coup de main projects. He should be able to reach his objective, perform the act of sabotage effectively, and either avoid detection or effect an escape. He should preferably be able to incite, organize, train, and lead sabotage groups.

– OSS Special Operations Field Manual, 23 February 1944

CHAPTER 3

Tools of the Trade

Research and Development

To accomplish their missions, SOE and OSS needed special equipment, with tools that were smaller, lighter, concealable, quieter or required for specific purposes. The standard equipment issued to the military was in certain cases adequate, but other items needed to be found and procured. If they did not already exist, they needed to be invented and built.

In April 1938, realising that war was coming, the head of SIS, Sir Hugh Sinclair, assigned one officer to head what would become Section D (D for devices). Major L. D. Grand, RE, had been charged to study sabotage – how to carry it out, develop methods and equipment for the task, how to train saboteurs and how to counter its use by the enemy. He was soon joined by another officer, Commander A. G. Langley, who set out to perfect initiators for explosive devices, including time fuses. One of the first items to be put into production was time pencils, devices that could be left unattended to detonate an explosive charge at a later time.

Nearly simultaneously, the War Department created an office called Military Intelligence Research, or MI(R), led by another Royal Engineer, Lieutenant Colonel 'Joe' Holland. He immediately brought in Major Millis Jefferis to head up a shop designated as MIR(c) to develop weapons and materials for irregular warfare.

SOE was created in July 1940 by combining SIS's Section D and MI(R) with Electra House. MIR(c), however, was separated from MI(R) and became MD1 within the Ministry of Defence in November 1940. It was later known as 'Churchill's Toy Shop' because of the Prime Minister's interests in its activities. MD1 was located at a house called The Firs in Whitchurch, Buckinghamshire. The SOE's integral Research & Development (R&D) offices were myriad and scattered through the English countryside.

Both offices developed a number of devious and useful items which found their way into the hands of SOE and OSS operatives, and of the resistance armies in the occupied territories.

Once again, the OSS came late to the game, and without the luxury of an existing office to subsume, director Donovan created the R&D Branch and chose Stanley P. Lovell to head it. Lovell was a chemist and business executive who had been working at the civilian National Development and Research Committee (NDRC). The NDRC's mission was to act as an advisory board for the development of new weapons for the military. His new job would be more specialised. Like SOE, the OSS R&D Branch would invent, develop and test material and equipment for special operations.

Unlike SOE, which often hired engineers and scientists and built its own research and production facilities, Lovell's branch worked extensively with private industry. Most of the fantastic gadgets were either perfected in laboratories like Kodak (the Beano grenade) or built by firms such as Southwest Pump Company (the US-version of the Welrod silent pistol), while Lovell and his band of inventors mostly confined themselves to conceptualising and developing the ideas to be put into production.

With success came failure. Among these were the Beano grenade, the search for a truth serum and an attempt to use insects to spread anthrax. Lovell was accepting of failures in the course of development, and stated, 'It was my policy to consider any method whatever that might aid the war, however unorthodox or untried.'

The Tools

Tools to Camouflage

Camouflage is more than making something invisible; it is also the art of deception. In the field of intelligence tradecraft it runs the gamut from producing false documentation that would fool a customs agent or policeman, to disguising a radio to make it look like a harmless object. Both the SOE and OSS required up-to-date documents to permit their undercover operatives freedom of travel in enemy-held areas. This meant they needed the best intelligence to tell them what the documents looked like, if changes were made and, of course, who needed what kind of papers to travel. Refugees were questioned about their documents, and their clothing was often exchanged for new in order to outfit an operative going into enemy territory. The underground was asked to provide details of any new documents or regulations to keep papers current.

Clothing that matched the type worn by the population of southern France might be different from that worn in Belgium – if an operative was arrested or searched, clothing had to match their persona. Clothing was sewn exactly as it would have been if it were made in the local area. And if a ration card suddenly changed, an 'authentic' fake had to be made to replace the old version. Details such as the print method, kind of paper and ink used, and methods of watermarking were of vital importance. Engraving and printing shops were established in London and Washington for the production of European and Asian documents, including passports, identity cards, work permits and licenses.

Deadly items such as explosives were often disguised as lumps of coal or rocks that would not raise suspicion. 'Dead letter drops', to facilitate two-way communications between operatives who could not physically speak to one another, were often designed to appear as disposed rubbish, a rock or even manure to hide secret messages. The artists quickly discovered that these items should not take the shape of anything edible or burnable, or they would be used as

Cover

Every operative and agent working in enemy, enemy-occupied or neutral territory must have a suitable cover – that is, an ostensibly legitimate reason for being where he is. Obviously, cover must be safe. That is, it must successfully shield the operative's secret activities. In the second place, it must allow the operative sufficient freedom of action to perform his mission. The activities of the operative must be consistent with his cover.

Cover is so important, and good covers so rare, that in many cases the finding of a good cover will determine the selection of the operative and the definition of his mission.

In the event of capture by the enemy, a secret intelligence operative or agent should stick by his cover story and deny all charges. Despite the seriousness of his own position, he should not fail to protect to the end the security of the organisation of which he is a member.

– OSS Secret Intelligence Manual, 22 March 1944

such if found. They also avoided shapes or materials that might be tempting to a child or a scrounger.

While field operatives and agents relied on their ingenuity and wits to survive, they had to be able to pass muster as a local from a distance as well as up close. To do that camouflage in all its forms – authentic clothing, documentation and everything they carried – was critical to keeping the operatives alive and their operations concealed from the enemy.

Tools to Communicate

Once an operative or a team was infiltrated into the operational area by sea, air or foot, one of the more difficult and risky tasks was to communicate over long distances. The ability to report information, request supplies or receive operational orders was

Lieutenant F. Ralph Ward and Morse code instructor John Balsamo operate a SSTR-1 radio at OSS Area C. (NARA, RG 226)

critical for individual operatives as well as the larger formations which were fielded by SOE and OSS. But just as they were crucial, radio communications were also an Achilles' heel for clandestine operations.

Several of SOE's missions collapsed when the Germans compromised operatives who failed to use proper security or when their codes and cyphers were captured and played back. Others were destroyed by traitors within the network. One of the most famous examples is the PROSPER circuit, and although it was believed a French member of the group, either Claude Dansey or Henri Déricourt, betrayed the circuit to the Germans, the truth remains unclear to this day.

One of the most critical factors in radio security was the length of time an operative remained on the air. Anything over 5 minutes was risky, as the Germans had mobile direction-finding (DF) units that could fix and pinpoint a transmitter given enough air time. Airtime would be reduced by using agreed-upon code words or numbers that indicated a longer message. Transmitting messages from the same spot was also deadly, as a number of operatives found out when German DF teams located their hide-out.

Radio procedures worked on a complex schedule that tried to optimise the best atmospherics for transmission as well as the best send times to minimise exposure. Operatives sent their messages on a schedule as a one-way 'blind transmission broadcast' (BTB) which did not require the receive station to acknowledge. Similarly, the operative or team would receive the home station's broadcast without coming up on the air. This reduced send time and the possibilities of being located by DF. Each station would acknowledge the other's messages in the next transmission.

In the beginning, SOE relied on SIS to give it the equipment and codes it needed. SIS naturally favoured its own operations over those of its 'cousin', and made life difficult. It wasn't until 1942 that SOE was better able to fend for itself by constructing its own compact radio sets with the help of engineers who were part of the exiled Polish government in Britain. Within a short while they had the A Mk I and II sets that were relatively compact – three small boxes that fitted in a small suitcase, as opposed to a large box weighing nearly 50lb. By the end of the war, SOE had a radio – the 51/1 – that weighed less than 6lb. The OSS used many of the SOE radios before they came up with their own, the SSTR-1, but it was the B Mk II which saw the most use throughout the war due to its ruggedness and reliability.

Beyond not getting caught with the radio at a checkpoint or in a barn loft after staying on the air for too long, security measures were required in the messages themselves. Colin Gubbins knew from experience that operations often failed when communications security was poor. He noted the security problems when he stated in *The Art of Guerilla Warfare*: 'ALL MESSAGES IN WIRELESS MUST BE IN CODE OR CIPHER.'

In training, operatives were taught a simple encoding system called the 'Playfair Cypher', but that system was not secure enough for actual use. Transposition systems based on a verse from a book or a poem were initially used, but were complicated and easily deciphered by an enemy that knew literature.

The best system was the One-Time Pad (OTP), which was a table of random letters in five-letter groups on a page. A message written over the groups was enciphered using a trigraph – a system of substitution by which a combination of two letters is replaced with a third. The resulting gibberish would be sent by Morse code and was unbreakable without the key. Only the holder of the copy of the same OTP page would be able to decode the message. Additionally, several security checks were inserted into messages that would thwart enemy attempts to deceive the home station if the operator, radio and OTP fell into the wrong hands. These were typically key words inserted at a specific point in the message. If that word was absent, the home base station knew that something was either wrong or the sender simply forgot. They would reply with an innocuous question to determine if the operator was under enemy control. The proper answer would allay suspicions. Unfortunately, either because of an oversight or a misguided willingness to overlook an 'error', home base did not always verify as they should have when the check word was omitted, which resulted in tragic consequences on several occasions.

Another code system developed by the first SOE operative dropped into France, Georges Bégué, codednamed BOMBPROOF, were the *messages personnels*, simple text messages transmitted over the high-power British Broadcasting Corporation network that only had a meaning to the agent receiving it.

Communications security was paramount and failures led to disasters. It was a combinations of errors, along with a penetration of a local cell, that destroyed the N (Netherlands) network and resulted in the deaths of nearly 60 SOE, SIS and MI9 operatives. *Unternehmen Nordpol* (Operation *Nord Pole*), the German playback of English communications, was one of the worst disasters, but not the only one, to befall SOE. Luckily, MI5's own playbacks and Operation *Ultra* more than compensated the Germans for their audacity.

The Germans could not decode any intercepted OTP messages, but that did not discourage SOE or OSS operators from routinely misreporting their actual location to prevent discovery in the event the enemy might be successful. (Later, special operators in Vietnam – among other locations – also took pains to do this, with the notable exception of calling in bombing missions, an instance that calls for precision.)

Of all the radio devices invented during World War II, one of the most innovative was the Rebecca/Eureka beacon system.

The system was designed to assist in more precise delivery of supplies to operatives and teams in occupied Europe. Before its invention, pilots had to rely on a navigator to plot their course by dead-reckoning and then find a small piece of open ground on a dark night where they would dump cargo, usually a parachute-borne cluster of packages and containers. If the crew was lucky, the drop zone (DZ) would be marked with lights or fires; if not, they had to guess. Often cargo went to the wrong location and was lost.

Dr R. Hanbury-Brown and J. W. S. Pringle of the British TRE (Telecommunications Research Establishment) came up with a solution. It consisted of a relatively small transponder called Eureka that would be set up on the DZ, and an airborne transceiver, Rebecca, in the airplane. As the aircraft approached the DZ, the transceiver would interrogate the ground unit transponder and receive a signal back that indicated distance and azimuth. With the system in operation, the accuracy of personnel and cargo drops improved greatly where it was used. Many resistance groups or operatives did not like the size and weight of Eureka, and simply abandoned or 'lost' the device. A smaller, lighter S-Phone that came into use later in the war was more popular. It permitted direct operative-to-aircraft radio communication that was not easy to intercept because of its highly directional antenna.

Sergeant William T. Alexander, flight engineer, with B-24D 'Playmate' of the 492nd BG 'Carpetbaggers' in 1944. Yagi antenna for Rebecca transponder on side of aircraft nose. (NARA/USAAF)

Tools to Kill

While SOE and OSS used all manner of conventional small arms in their operations, they eschewed heavy weapons or artillery as it tended to tie the guerrilla or operative to one location. They preferred lighter, more mobile weapons like the Bren machine gun, the M-1 and M-2 carbine, the .45 calibre M1911 Colt automatic pistol, the PIAT (Projector Infantry Anti-Tank) and the 60mm mortar. But specialised weapons were also required. The following lists a few of the most useful and a few that just didn't work out.

Fairbairn-Sykes Fighting Knife

Probably the most well-recognised piece of kit used by SOE and OSS is the F-S Fighting Knife. In 1940, while in the employ of the SOE

in England, William Fairbairn and
Eric Sykes designed a knife suitable for their methods of killing. It
was designed not to 'fight', but to
kill quickly. Lighter and thinner
than most existing military knives,
it had both a sharp point and
cutting edges. It was thin enough
to penetrate thick clothing and
slide through the ribs to produce
a clean, deep wound that would
bleed heavily. The first pattern
knives were made by Wilkinson
Sword; thereafter they were made
by many companies in the UK. The
knives were used in great numbers
by the SOE, Commandos, SBS
and SAS during the war. The OSS
adopted a version after its encounters with Fairbairn at Camp X. The
third pattern F-S knife was the

The Fairbairn-Sykes 1st Pattern
Fighting Knife. (Author's collection)

final version and was optimised for large-scale industrial production
over the labour-intensive first and second patterns. It is still issued
to British Commandos.

There was also a version that is today known as the 'OSS Stiletto'.
After the Fairbairn-Sykes was adopted by the OSS, its manufacture
was contracted out to the housewares manufacturer Landers, Frary
and Clark of New Britain, Connecticut. The knives were issued with
an unusual sheath adapted from the company's existing stocks of
metal kitchen spatulas.

Stinger

The T1E1 Stinger was a one-shot .22 calibre concealment weapon. It
could be worn in a shirt breast pocket as a 'writing utensil'. It was a

tiny and easily concealed weapon for close ranges. It could easily be fired from the palm of the hand at a person while sitting in a room or passing in a crowd. Inexpensive and available in large quantities, the gun could easily be distributed widely in occupied countries. It could not be reloaded and was discarded after use. Ten pens were packed in a wood and cardboard box sealed in a moisture-proof envelope. The Stinger gun measured 3½in in length and ½in in diameter, and weighed 1oz.

Although it was used for self-protection and assassinations, it was also seen as a tool to acquire military weapons from the enemy – sort of a 'shoot one, get one' kind of deal.

Stanley P. Lovell, head of OSS R&D, related the story of a how a Stinger saved an OSS operative:

> An OSS agent was picked up by the Gestapo inside the German lines. The German security officer was in doubt about him, something in his story or manner didn't quite fit his ostensible calling. They frisked him and found no weapon, but the officer put him in a staff car. Being unarmed, our man rode on the back seat with the security officer. They were en route to German headquarters for further interrogation. In a small village the officer got out to telephone ahead and assure himself that a certain interrogator would be called in.
>
> Our OSS agent, left alone with the military chauffeur in the front seat, took out the overlooked Stinger, cocked it, held it near the back of the driver's head and fired. He pushed the body to one side, took over the wheel and drove at breakneck speed to the American line.
>
> The Stinger not only saved the man's life but allowed our planes to destroy the German Headquarters where he was to be taken. By telling the driver what route to take, the security officer had unwittingly given the OSS man priceless information. A little Stinger is a dangerous thing.

Lovell was given to hyperbole, but a German account (Holger Eckhertz, *D-Day Through German Eyes*, DTZ, 2016) shows how the underground put the Stinger to use. On the night of the D-Day invasion, a German officer was invited by a young French woman to a room in a French country inn. When the officer was missed the next morning a search party found him face down on the formerly white sheets of the bed, now red with his blood. He was dead, his

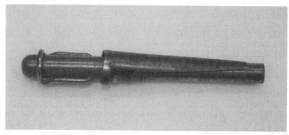

T1E1 Stinger Single Use Concealment Weapon. (US Army Center for Military History)

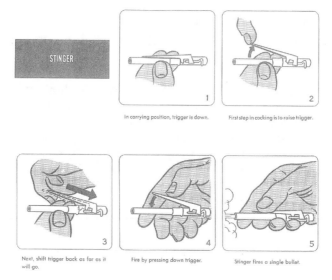

In carrying position, trigger is down.

First step in cocking is to raise trigger.

Next, shift trigger back as far as it will go.

Fire by pressing down trigger.

Stinger fires a single bullet.

T1E1 Stinger instructions from OSS Weapons Catalog, 1943. (NARA, RG 226)

brains splattered on the wall. A Stinger was found in the room, its one round expended. The woman had disappeared.

Thousands of the devices were dropped into France for the resistance. However they were used, the name was appropriate for those on its wrong end.

Colt Model 1903 Pocket Hammerless Pistol

Both OSS and SOE operatives carried this .32 caliber pistol in the field. Designed by John Browning and produced by the Colt Patent

Firearms Manufacturing Company, prior to WWII it was a favorite of everyone from the Shanghai Municipal Police to the gangster John Dillinger. During the war many were given to members of the resistance, including Frédéric "Alain" Laboureur, a French *Maquisard* who carried one during the battle of Mont Mouchet.

A Colt Model 1903 issued to the SOE in WWII. (Courtesy of OldColt.com)

Welrod MkI 9mm silenced pistol. (Courtesy of Anders Thygesen, http://www.timelapse.dk)

The SOE versions are generally identifiable by the lack of a "US Government Property" (having been obliterated with punch struck 'X's') and they are painted with matte black enamel paint over the original parkerized finish. There was also a "close quarter assassination" belt mounted version designed to be worn under the operative's clothing with the pistol on the right hip aiming forward. It was fired by a remote cable trigger mechanism.

Welrod Silenced Pistol

The Welrod was born in the creative workshops of Station IX, invented by a one of its 'mad' scientists, Major Hugh Q. A. Reeves. This pistol was just one of his many inventions, but perhaps the most deadly. It was given a code name beginning with 'Wel-' like all the devices developed at Station IX; the 'Wel-' deriving from the Station's proximity to the village of Welwyn, about an hour north of London.

The first Welrod was chambered for .32 caliber ACP ammunition and was used by the SOE and Danish underground. A later version chambered for 9mm Parabellum was adopted by the OSS. The weapon is manually operated and can fire a single shot, after which a new round is loaded by twisting the rear knob and pulling the bolt back. Pushing forward strips a round from the magazine and feeds it into the chamber. The knob is twisted and locked, which cocks the weapon for firing. A simple grip safety blocks the trigger but not the firing pin. The pistol weight is 48oz, with an overall length of 14½in.

The Welrod was designed from the beginning to be silent. It has a barrel perforated with 16–20 holes that is surrounded by a metal tube containing an expansion chamber and a perforated metal ring, which leads to the silencer section consisting of 18 metal discs and rubber baffles. The rubber baffles allow the fired projectile to pass through, then close up behind it. The silencer section is designed to be replaceable as a unit. The pistol's hand grip and magazine detach from the gun as a unit, permitting the weapon to be better concealed. Tests indicated that the sound of its firing was approximately 78db, making it one of the quietest pistols ever produced.

Although the Welrod was meant to be used 'up close', it was effective to around 25 metres. After that, the reduced muzzle velocity and the short barrel began to take its toll on accuracy. The training manual noted that the weapon was best used 'with the muzzle against the target'. It also noted that 'no special training' was necessary for this manoeuvre. One would assume, however, that a great deal of nerve would be required.

Production of the Welrod began in 1943 at the Birmingham Small Arms (BSA) Company, with later production taking place at other factories throughout England. The exact number of pistols produced remains a mystery, although some historians believe that as many as 14,000 were made. Many were air-dropped to resistance movements in Denmark and the Netherlands. The US also produced an unknown number of Welrods for the OSS. Most Welrods were completely unmarked; a sterile weapon, theoretically untraceable to the originating country.

High Standard HDM Suppressed Pistol

Although the Welrod was an excellent silent pistol, its slow reload procedure meant it was not the best choice for an operative who might need to fire several rounds rapidly. For that situation there was a better weapon: the High Standard HDMS.

The High Standard Manufacturing Company was established in 1926. At the outbreak of World War II, the US War Department purchased High Standard's pistols as a low-cost training device. When the OSS began to develop suppressed pistols, it first used the Colt Woodsman and the H-S Model B. The Woodsman proved too long and the Model B was replaced by the H-D in 1942. The military version was dubbed the Model 'HDM' and became the base for an OSS modified weapon called the 'HDMS' ('S' for suppressed).

With an overall length of 13¼ in, it weighed just less than 3lb unloaded and had a 10-round magazine. Bell Telephone Laboratories developed a suppressor which encased the 6¾in barrel, which was drilled to allow the gases from the fired cartridge to escape into the suppressor. The pistol was also fitted with a slide lock that prevented gases from escaping from the action. The suppressor is made up of a roll of tin-coated brass mesh screen in the rear compartment, while the front contains 85 bronze washers. The pistol had an effective range of 50 yards, although it performed best at short range.

The suppressor could reduce the pistol's report to the level of a person whispering. The suppressor had a lifespan of around 200 rounds before it needed to be replaced. Approximately 2,500 HDMS pistols were produced.

Suppressed M-3 Sub-machine Gun

Silenced or suppressed pistols are great tools, but sometimes more firepower is called for. The US already had a sub-machine gun available – the .45 calibre M-3, aka the 'Grease-gun' because of its similarity to the tool. Because of this, all R&D had to do was develop a barrel assembly for the weapon that would quieten its firing.

It was impossible to achieve total elimination of noise in an automatic weapon such as the M-3 because of the recoil operated action, but R&D was able to effect a 90 per cent sound reduction. In the case of the M-3, all that was necessary was to unscrew the old barrel and replace it with the R&D one.

Developed by Bell Laboratories, the assembly consists of a drilled gun barrel and a two-stage silencing chamber surrounding and extending beyond the gun barrel muzzle. Along its length, the gun barrel has 48 holes in four straight rows. During firing, gases are bled off through the holes, with a consequent reduction in the gas pressure and muzzle velocity. Although the suppresser quietened the initial 'pop' and muzzle noise, the mechanical action remained quite loud.

Some users preferred the suppressed Sten, known as the MkII(S), because it was quieter and could be disassembled into a small package, and its 9mm ammunition was considerably lighter (and more available) than the M-3's .45 calibre ammo, but the M-3 was more reliable and had better 'knockdown' power.

De Lisle Carbine

Between the silenced and suppressed pistols and the barely suppressed sub-machine gun came the De Lisle carbine, a bolt-action, .45 ACP calibre, suppressed short rifle. It was developed from the standard British No. 1 Mk III SMLE by William Godfrey De Lisle. Because it was manually cycled with its bolt action, there was no mechanical cycling sound as with the suppressed Sten or M-3. With a reported muzzle noise of 85.5db, it was quieter than the sub-machine guns and more accurate than the pistols, with a longer effective range and better lethality. The rifle used a shortened SMLE bolt mechanism and was re-chambered to take the .45 calibre pistol ammunition. It was quietened with an integral 2in diameter suppressor around a modified and ported 9in-long Thompson SMG barrel. Of the 600 weapons originally ordered, the Sterling Armaments Company is believed to have produced less than 200 during World

War II. Several stories of its use in Europe to 'take out' senior German officers have surfaced, but none have been confirmed.

Beano Grenade developed by OSS and manufactured by Kodak. (International Military Antiques)

Beano Grenade

In the 'not everything works as planned' category is the T-13 hand grenade. Developed by the OSS and produced by the Eastman Kodak Company, it was called the 'Beano' because it was the same size and weight as a baseball. An underlying assumption was that any young American male could throw it accurately. It had both a pressure trigger and an in-flight arming device. The grenade was designed to be thrown as a traditional baseball, and as such it was held with two fingers on a weighted and knurled cap, and the arming pin was removed. Once thrown, the cap detached from the body of the grenade and a secondary arming pin primed the grenade to detonate upon impact. It weighed a total of 12oz with its Composition A explosive charge. Several thousand of the grenades were manufactured, but most were recalled when several exploded prematurely during testing.

Tools for Sabotage

'Widespread practice of simple sabotage will harass and demoralize enemy administrators and police.'

– OSS SIMPLE SABOTAGE MANUAL

Sabotage is the deliberate act of subversion, disruption or destruction to weaken a government or military organisation. It can take place through simple work slowdowns, stuffing cigarettes into the fuel lines of a Tiger tank as it is being built, cutting telegraph wires or, in the extreme, blowing up a train. Sabotage is extremely effective, but can have consequences that must always be considered. Those range from the impact of an act on the general population, e.g. contaminating the water supply, to retribution by the enemy against innocent civilians. The following are some of the 'toys' developed or improved by SOE and OSS during the war.

Caltrop

One of the simplest and oldest of sabotage tools, the caltrop is a spiked metal device thrown on the ground to impede the movement of men, cavalry horses or wheeled vehicles. Known to the Romans and Genghis Khan, the caltrop was made in large numbers and parachuted to Resistance fighters in Europe for use against German convoys. Made of steel, it was shaped so that when

Caltrop used by the OSS. The hollow spikes puncture self-sealing rubber tyres. The hole in the centre allows air to escape even if the other end of the tube is sealed by soft ground. (CIA, Office of the Historian)

it was dropped on a road, there were three prongs or legs pointing downward and one that stood erect. About 3in high and weighing only 1oz, it would cause a tyre to blowout if run over. An improvement to the design by the R&D shop was to make the caltrop with hollow tubes that allowed the air to quickly escape from a punctured tyre. If stepped on, the result was a devastating injury to man or animal.

Plastic Explosive

Not invented by SOE, but certainly used successfully during many operations by both SOE and OSS, one of the first military plastic explosives was known as Nobel's Explosive No. 808. It was developed in Britain just in time for World War II. It was shared with the United States in September 1940 by the Tizard Mission – officially the British Technical and Scientific Mission – and quickly found its way into large-scale production and the hands of the OSS. *Plastique* (as the French call it) is a soft, pliable explosive suitable for engineering or sabotage demolitions; it can be moulded into a needed shape to cut metal or destroy concrete. It was used throughout the war by operatives of both organisations, as well as the resistance. Captured British Nobel 808 was used in the failed assassination attempt on Adolf Hitler at his Wolf's Lair headquarters in Eastern Prussia (Operation *Valkyrie*).

Time Pencil

The time pencil delay was one of the most important sabotage tools used during the war. It had been invented by the Germans during World War I and was improved by the Poles after the war. Gubbins acquired some of the devices in the spring of 1939 when he was in Poland, and SOE would subsequently improve the device further. When demand increased, SOE provided plans to the OSS, who arranged for the manufacture of thousands of the devices. The devices came in several forms.

The earliest form was the acid delay (also called SRA-2 and SRA-3), which consisted of a capsule with a thin wire inside that held back a spring-activated striker. When the delay's tube was crushed, acid was released and would eat away at the wire until it broke. The pencil came in boxes of five and a set consisted of six boxes, each coded with different colours to indicate the approximate length of the delay. The delay was dependent on two factors: the wire thickness and the ambient temperature. The colder the environment, the longer the delay; while hot temperatures sped up the process. The delay was timed for 6 minutes at the minimum and 20 hours at the maximum.

The L-Delay worked with a Tellurium lead cylinder inside a tube that was put under tension by a spring when the safety pin was removed. The lead cylinder stretched at a uniform rate, and when it broke it released the striker. This delay was more accurate, but was only produced in small numbers and used primarily by SOE.

A-C Delay was developed by SOE and was based on a celluloid washer that retained a firing pin. When activated, acetone was released from a crushed ampoule and dissolved the washer, which released the firing pin. Delays on these devices ranged from 4½ hours to eight weeks. It was used predominantly with the underwater Limpet mines.

When more accuracy was needed, a clockwork fuse was employed. There were also delay detonators that were activated by air pressure changes and used for sabotaging aircraft in flight.

No. 10 Time pencil fuses and plastic explosive with fuse and blasting cap. (Courtesy of Anders Thygesen, http://www.timelapse.dk)

Firefly

This was an ingeniously small incendiary device designed to be dropped in the gasoline tank of a vehicle. The gasoline would cause two rubber washers to swell and withdraw a plunger that would, in turn, release a spring-loaded firing pin. The firing pin would detonate a small explosive charge that would burst the gas tank and ignite the contents. The delay was 2–7 hours, depending again on temperature.

'Aunt Jemima' Exploding Flour

In December 1942, Lovell sent a classified letter to Dr E. M. Chadwell at the NDRC requesting a curious formula for 'an edible mixture of flour and RDX'. Flour and RDX (Research Department Explosive) were mixed to create something that looked and acted like regular baking flour, but which with the addition of a blasting cap would have 'a greater explosive force than TNT'. It could be made into bread, biscuits or cake and eaten, because RDX was non-toxic. Saboteurs could use it dry, as dough or in baked form. Once baked, it appeared to be an innocuous loaf of bread or muffin. The saboteur merely inserted a detonator and placed the 'bread' where it would do the most damage when it exploded.

As soon as the formula began to be produced and packaged to look like commercial flour, it acquired the name 'Aunt Jemima' after the American pre-packaged pancake mix available at the time. It was reported that 15 tons of the flour mix was used in the China-Burma-India (CBI) theatre alone.

Coal

Exploding coal's first documented use was in the American Civil War (1861–65) and was developed by Captain Thomas Edgeworth Courtenay of the Confederate Secret Service. Its use was resurrected by the OSS and was actually more of a disguise mechanism than a new product. In some cases lumps of real coal were hollowed out and filled with explosive, while in others a mix of TNT explosive and stabiliser were formed into 'coal' nuggets. The idea was to place the devices into fuel bins, where it would be shovelled in the boiler of a train locomotive or similar engine. Once heated up, the coal would explode, destroying the engine and hopefully the crew.

Limpet

The Limpet was a small self-contained explosive mine equipped with magnets to hold it in place on the hull of an enemy ship or an iron or steel target on land such as a tank. Designed by Colonel Stuart Macrae and Cecil Vandepeer Clarke, who were with MIR(c) at the time, the mine was filled with 3½lb of high explosive that could penetrate a 60mm-thick metal plate. It was detonated using either a No. 9 'L' or the No. 8 pencil timer. The magnets even kept it in place on a ship cruising at 16 knots. The magnets could be removed if desired. The total weight was less than 5lb without the

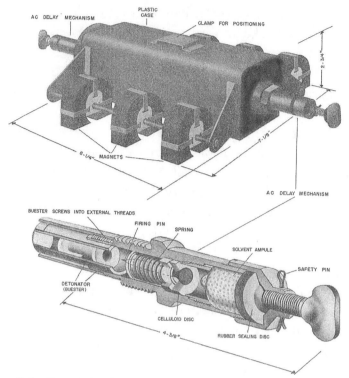

Limpet Delay Fuse A.C. Mk I with various time delay ampoules and carrying tin. (Courtesy of David Sampson @ MillsGrenades.co.uk)

magnets and 10lb with them attached. OSS's R&D section designed a similar device.

Field experience later demonstrated the necessity for some other method of attachment, since in certain cases barnacles on the hulls prevented the Limpets from sticking. R&D therefore developed the 'Pin-Up Girl' – a device that delivered a hardened steel nail into the plates of the ship by an explosive cartridge to hold the Limpet in place.

One of the most successful uses of the mine was during Operation *Jaywick*, conducted by the Z Special Unit of the Australian Services Reconnaissance Department (SRD) – formerly the Inter-Allied Services Department (ISD). During the operation, a joint unit of

Schematic drawing of a Limpet mine and fuse ignitor. (NARA, RG 226)

British and Australian special operators placed Limpets on Japanese ships in Singapore harbour, sinking seven and damaging over 30,000 tonnes of shipping.

Carborundum

SOE operative Anthony Brooks, code named 'Alphonse', set up a resistance network in southern France. When the D-Day invasion began, his PIMENTO teams were tasked with delaying German reinforcements from reaching Normandy. They successfully held up the movements of the 2nd SS Panzer *Das Reich* Division that had been refitting near Toulouse. He sent two teenage girls, one 16 and the other 14, into rail yards to siphon off the axle oil from the division's rail transport cars, replacing it with carborundum abrasive grease which, as soon as the cars started moving, caused the axles to seize and rendered them immobile. Forced onto the roads, the German tanks slowly made their way north, encountering a series of resistance force ambushes initiated by George Starr's WHEELWRIGHT network. The combination of sabotage and raids slowed the division's momentum and ensured it was not able to reach the front lines until D+17, too late to defeat the landings. Both Starr and Brooks were awarded the DSO and MC.

The list goes on, for the engineers and scientists loved to devise implements of destruction that would be effective and useful to operatives in the field. Not all of them made it off the drawing boards, but those that did were worth the effort. Many of the ideas and their spin-offs are still in use today.

Still Valid Today – The Target Analysis Process

A common acronym used for target analysis is CARVER: criticality, accessibility, recuperability, vulnerability, effect and recognisability. First developed by the OSS, this acronym captures the criteria which analyse a target.

   a. Criticality. Criticality, or target value, is the primary consideration in targeting. A target is critical when its destruction or damage would significantly impair an enemy's political, economic, or military operations.

   b. Accessibility. In order to damage, destroy, or conduct surveillance of a target, operatives must be able to reach it, either physically or via indirect weapons means.

   c. Recuperability. In the case of sabotage missions, it is important to estimate how long it will take the enemy to repair, replace, or bypass the damage inflicted on the target. Recuperability is a vital supporting element of criticality. A target may not be lucrative for SOE employment if it can be repaired, replaced, or bypassed in a short time with minimum resources.

   d. Vulnerability. A target is vulnerable if SOE have the means and expertise to conduct the planned mission and achieve the desired level of damage or other objectives as assigned.

e. Effect. For targets of more purely military value, the impact of both attacking (or surveilling) the target and achieving the desired results must be assessed. The mission must be evaluated as well as the impact of target destruction on the health and welfare of the indigenous civilian population.

f. Recognisability. The target must be identifiable under various weather, light, and seasonal conditions and configurations (if applicable) without being confused with other targets or target components.

– Joint Pub 3 – 05.5, 10 August 1993

CHAPTER 4

Operations

'Surprise, Kill, and Vanish'

– MOTTO OF THE JEDBURGHS

Shortly after Churchill ordered SOE to 'set Europe ablaze', it received its first directive from the Chiefs of Staff to begin operations on 25 November 1940. Insertions into Europe began quickly, but not all would go well. Under pressure to accomplish something, the early missions were often organised and launched precipitously. Failures were expected. Slowly, the SOE gained experience and improved. Soon, the American OSS would follow, looking for its own 'chance to raise merry hell'.

Throughout the war their missions ran the gamut from singleton operatives collecting vital intelligence to small teams undertaking large-scale raids on German, Italian and Japanese military targets. Some of the objectives were tactical, such as bridges that carried troops or supplies to the front, the destruction of which would affect the local situation. Some were strategic: collecting enemy defence plans, killing an enemy VIP or sabotaging factories that produced components critical to the war effort.

The methods, tactics, techniques and procedures used were developed as an understanding of the operational environment evolved. Each situation generally required a unique approach. Challenges and problems were analysed and solved using different methods. In short, flexibility, adaptability and independent thinking were required to achieve success.

Getting to the operational area in the first place required unique resources, which for SOE initially meant relying on assistance from either the Royal Air Force or the Royal Navy. In early 1941, Britain's priority was to bomb Germany and destroy its industrial capacity. SOE was to support that strategy on the ground through sabotage. The most significant constraint, beyond the number of trained operatives, was the availability of aircraft. SOE had to fight with the RAF over the aircraft, which Bomber Command argued were needed for the strategic bombing effort. In May 1942, SOE was limited to operations in Western Europe and Scandinavia, while support for Poland and Czechoslovakia was restricted. It was a logistical 'battle' that would continue throughout the war.

In the beginning, the goal of training and organising secret armies in Europe was reduced to a minimum because of the lack of air resources. Despite Churchill's desire to 'set Europe ablaze', the need for aircraft would initially inhibit activities.

Slowly, specialised units were set up to transport the operatives and equipment needed. Two RAF units, 138 and 161 Special Duties Squadrons, were set up at Tempsford Airfield in Bedfordshire to support SOE. Formed from the RAF Number 419 Special Duties Flight, they used a range of aircraft, starting with Armstrong Whitworth Whitleys and Douglas Havocs, then Handley Page Halifax and Short Stirling bombers, as well as the venerable Westland Lysander liaison aircraft. The Lysander 'Taxi' would prove invaluable to insert and pick up operatives from small fields in the dead of night – something the big bombers and transports could not manage.

By the war's end, 12 additional squadrons would be activated to assist in England, while the RAF's 148 and 624 Squadrons operated out of Italy and Algeria respectively. Less known are the airmen and aircraft of the 357 Special Duties Squadron which operated out of India and served SOE operations in Burma.

The OSS initially had to make do with jumping from conventional RAF aircraft, but slowly developed its own resources, first with three

Lysander on improvised airstrip at Bolo Auk in Burma. (TNA HS 7/107 – Burma)

B-17s in what was called the Special Flight Section based in Algeria that flew operatives into southern France.

When the American 801st/492nd Bombardment Group, known as the 'Carpetbaggers', arrived at Harrington Airfield in Northamptonshire they were equipped with modified B-24 bombers. Additional special mission aircraft were used for certain operations (reconnaissance and insertion), including the A-26 and C-47, along with several Mosquito, Norseman, Stirling and Wellington airplanes. Just prior to D-Day, the 'Carpetbagger' squadron had 64 B-24 aircraft at its disposal.

Other forms of transport were needed in addition to aircraft. Operations in Norway were supported by a special maritime unit called the 'Shetland Bus' – officially the Norwegian Naval Independent Unit (NNIU) – that used Norwegian fishing boats to infiltrate operatives and teams into Norway. The unit was augmented with three former US Navy 110ft sub-chasers in 1943.

Submarines were used for some infiltrations, but the risk of losing such a valuable vessel drove the search for an alternative. The OSS Maritime Unit (MU) eventually acquired Motor Torpedo Boats (MTBs), sometimes called 'Fast Boats', to infiltrate and exfiltrate teams.

The embryonic nature of the resistance in Europe also slowed operations. The communists were the only group in France reasonably trained to oppose the German occupation at the beginning of the war because they had experience surviving as an underground organisation. The *Francs-Tireurs et Partisans* (FTP) was the first to come into existence. Even then, only a few communists opposed Germany before Hitler attacked the Soviet Union and broke the Treaty of Non-aggression. Even without SOE support, the resistance grew as more people realised the nature of the German occupation and felt the only recourse was struggle.

Politics heavily influenced where and with whom the Allies conducted unconventional operations. The parts of Eastern Europe occupied by the Soviet Union were off-limits to SOE and OSS because Stalin wanted no outside interference in his area of influence. And to varying degrees, the OSS was often more willing than the SOE to work with communist guerrillas, despite the expectation of post-war political difficulties in the liberated areas.

Under Winston Churchill's directives, SOE worked with the Greek People's Liberation Army (ELAS), the guerrilla arm of the communist party (EAM), as well as the republican National Republican Greek League (EDES), while in Yugoslavia, SOE worked first with the right-wing Chetnik partisans, then switched to support Josip Broz ('Tito') and his communist partisans when it was discovered the Chetniks were supportive of the Germans.

France posed its own problems for SOE and required two country sections to run operations: 'RF' for the General Charles de Gaulle-aligned resistance, and 'F' for the independent resistance, along with several smaller sections. SOE had to control over 400 operatives sent into France while balancing the precarious egos of French leaders who sought personal control of the various resistance groups. Later, with the deployment of the Operation *Jedburgh* teams to support D-Day (discussed below), a unified office called the *État-major des Forces Françaises de l'Intérieur* (EMFFI) was set up to control inter-allied operations.

Operational responsibilities were divided between the SOE and OSS along regional lines. As SOE had established itself in Europe, including the Balkans, OSS acceded to a secondary role there. It would assist British operations but was not to initiate any of its own without close consultations. In theory, OSS took the lead in North-west Africa, China and the Pacific, while SOE held primacy almost everywhere else. In Germany and Italy, both claimed independence of their operations. In practice, there was a good deal of competition and not a little acrimony between two wartime organisations manned and commanded by alpha males.

In September 1942, a joint UK/US office called SOE/SO – informally known as 'The London Group' (after 1 May 1944, it became Special Force Headquarters, SFHQ) – was set up in London to work with the theatre command, Supreme Headquarters Allied Expeditionary Forces (SHAEF), to:

1. promote resistance in occupied countries;
2. arm and equip resistance groups;
3. give direction to resistance groups;
4. plan actions to be taken by resistance groups; and
5. coordinate actions of resistance groups with Allied military plans.

In the Mediterranean, a similar attempt to coordinate operations was made with the Special Operations Mediterranean (SOM) office at the Allied Force Headquarters (AFHQ). SOM, which had the cover name Force 133, set up sub-elements Force 266, to operate in Yugoslavia, Greece and Albania, and Force 139 for Poland and Czechoslovakia.

While cooperation worked well in London, in the Mediterranean theatre it had mixed results because of differing political views

French circuit operatives 'suit up' for their insertion into France. (492nd Bombing Group Files, US Air War College Archives)

and an American perception that SOE wanted to keep OSS at a subordinate level. Although there were exceptions, after Italy and for the remainder of the war, the two organisations mostly worked together for success in Europe and the Far East.

The Missions

World War II presented the Allies with many challenges and opportunities. While conventional ground, naval and air forces would prove critical, unconventional forces would also play a role – sometimes small, sometimes pivotal – in the eventual victory over the Axis.

As noted earlier, SOE and OSS conducted irregular warfare that consisted of diverse activities: raids on strategic targets, elimination of key military leaders and intelligence collection to support the overall war effort.

One of their most important roles, however, was to support the underground, resistance, or partisan groups that were fighting the enemy on their own home ground. The Allies provided assistance in many areas, from airdropping vital supplies such as weapons, explosives and radios, to providing on-the-ground leadership and technical advice, and augmenting guerrilla forces for combat missions.

It is useful, therefore, to briefly outline the classical components of the resistance forces that fought in Norway, France, Yugoslavia, Italy, Greece, Burma and elsewhere around the globe during the war.

The Underground: a secret network responsible for subversion, sabotage, intelligence collection and other activities that could not be undertaken by the guerrillas. Because most underground operations took place in and around cities, the members of this group often used false identities and closely mixed with the population and the enemy. SOE and OSS gave the name 'circuits' to their teams attached to the networks.

The Guerrillas: the armed element of the resistance who generally remained hidden from the enemy and the population, coming out only to strike. It was the guerrilla who conducted most of the armed combat against the enemy. The JEDBURGHs, OGs and Inter-Allied Teams worked with these elements.

The Auxiliary: the primary support wing of the resistance. Although they might not have played an active, day-to-day role, they worked to support the movement by providing early warning, manning safe houses and supplying intelligence and logistical support.

It is important to remember that a resistance group generally followed several steps in its formation. First, it must prepare and develop prior to taking on any military or offensive operations. This entailed recruiting and training trustworthy personnel and the collection of intelligence. It must be able to communicate securely among its members, and it must set up counter-intelligence methods to protect itself from compromise or penetration by the enemy or traitors. Internal security of the groups was vital and many circuits were compromised by traitors as well as communications failures.

When the group reached operational status, small-scale acts of resistance came first; for example, painting propaganda messages on a wall or cutting telephone lines. More elaborate or dangerous acts like bombings or assassination could also take place, but the organisation must always consider how the enemy or the people would react. The question that must be asked was: would enemy retribution reduce local support for the resistance or would it galvanise support?

A build-up phase followed, characterised by continued small-scale operations, recruitment, training and expansion of all capabilities, especially intelligence collection on enemy strength, locations, activities and capabilities. As has been said, if you don't know your enemy, you will be overcome in battle.

Small-scale operations like ambushes, sabotage and assassinations took place when the resistance was confident it could carry out the mission and disappear without being caught in a set-piece battle. Surprise, speed and violence of action are hallmarks of a good operation, but at this stage the ability to get away and survive another day was paramount if the resistance was to survive.

Large-scale combat operations began only when the guerrilla organisation felt it was not only ready to succeed – but able to meet any enemy countermove. If the resistance faced off against a strong enemy too soon, it risked destruction. A failure in battle meant going back to square one and beginning again – a waste of effort, time and lives.

Generally, in Western Europe, most large-scale guerrilla or resistance operations did not begin until just before Allied conventional forces landed on the coast. In other locations like the Balkans and Burma, such operations were possible only when the enemy was in difficult terrain or isolated positions.

SOE's and, by extension, OSS' two-phase strategy meant they needed two kinds of operatives. For the first 'build-up' phase, they needed men and women – some civilian, some military – mostly locals who could speak the local language fluently, could carry off a cover with the proper identification, clothing and knowledge, and could live a life clandestinely under pressure. They were generally grouped in three-person teams – an organiser, deputy/courier and W/T operator – which would infiltrate the target area and organise what were called 'circuits'. The circuit's primary mission was to build up the underground and to support what would come later – organised resistance. As JEDBURGH historian Will Irwin points out, women often filled this role more easily than men because they could move about a village or travel without raising suspicions, while a fit, military-aged male would invite questions from the police or security forces. The British had at least 40 female circuit operatives. While the OSS infiltrated several French women resistance members, they had but one trained American woman in the field – Virginia Hall, MBE, DSC, *Croix de Guerre avec Palme*.

The second group of operatives were those who would work with the armed resistance or guerrilla force. These were operatives who generally did not need to pass themselves off as locals. They operated as members of a military unit – the resistance – and needed to have mastered the profession of arms in order to give advice or lead a unit in combat. That meant they were all soldiers and all males.

The number and scope of SOE and OSS operations cannot be fully detailed in this short history, but the mission vignettes that follow touch on many of the aspects discussed above and give a taste of how the men and women operatives worked and what they accomplished.

Gathering Intelligence and Building the Resistance

First In: Georges Bégué (SOE)

Georges Bégué was serving in the French Army when war broke out in 1939. With the rapid onslaught of German forces, he found himself at Dunkirk and was one of the few French soldiers evacuated to England. He wanted to continue his service and was eventually recruited in 1941 as a 'pianist' – a radio operator – in SOE's 'F'

Section. Trained in England and Scotland, he was codenamed 'Bombproof', having narrowly avoided being killed in a Nazi air attack on London, and given the alias identity George Noble.

Bégué became the first SOE agent to be successfully parachuted into France with a radio on the night of 5/6 May 1941 in the Varan region between the towns of Vierzon and Chateauroux. He was dropped 'blind,' that is without a reception party on the ground to welcome him. He had to walk to the home of his first contact, Max Hymans, a former parliamentarian. He quickly went to work in support of the resistance and eventually joined AUTOGIRO network as its radio operator. The Germans put a lot of resources into detecting the resistance, and one of the SOE's weak points was the use of radios. Radio Detection equipment, including mobile vans, made it difficult for the operators to stay on the air for more than a few minutes and they had to change their transmit locations often.

While in the field, Bégué proposed that the SOE use the powerful transmitters of the British Broadcasting Corporation to send messages in clear language that sounded nonsensical but would have

Georges Bégué. (Famille Bégué)

a specific meaning to the agent that received them. In September 1941, the first *message personnelles, Lisette va bien* (Lisette is OK), was sent out over BBC.

Despite some initial successes at organization, if not operations, the SOE agents continued to be pursued by the Gestapo and the *Abwehr*, the German internal security organs, and bad luck doomed Bégué's cell. Another group of SOE agents were infiltrated into France on 10 October 1942. One of them, Denis Tuberville, was quickly arrested by *Vichy Sûreté* (police) with the address of a safehouse in his pocket. With the address, the Vichy were able to set up a 'mousetrap' at the safehouse, the Villa des Bois address in Châteauroux, to arrest any SOE agents who showed up. The trick worked and six agents, including George Bégué, were arrested – Bégué on 24 October 1942. They were sent to the Vichy prison Mauzac where they encountered several more SOE agents who had also been captured.

The Vichy unwisely allowed one of the prisoners, a French SOE agent named Jean Pierre-Bloch, contact with his wife, Gabrielle Sadourny Bloch. Over the course of several weeks, Madam Bloch along with one of the few remaining SOE operatives in France, Virginia Hall, managed to put together an escape plan. An ambitious plan, it involved the suborning of several guards, the manufacture of a gate key, and Bloch's wife smuggling wire-cutters and tools in the care packages she was allowed to bring into the prison. In the early morning hours of 16 July 1942, 12 agents escaped the prison. Making their way on foot cross county, they were then taken in a truck to a safehouse deep in a forest where they waited until the search was called off. Miss Hall had planted the story that the prisoners had all been picked up by British aircraft and flown to England. After two weeks, the group made its way in twos and threes across the border into Spain and thence to England.

Bégué was decorated with the Military Cross and was appointed 'F' Section Signals Officer under Maurice Buckmaster. He emigrated to the United States after the war and died in 1993, at age 81, survived by his wife Rosemary and two daughters, Brigitte and Suzanne.

The White Rabbit: Wing Commander F. F. Edward Yeo-Thomas (SOE)

Edward Yeo-Thomas came to SOE in 1942 with a great deal of experience. Born in London but raised in France, he served in World War I as a dispatch rider and then fought in the Polish-Soviet War before being captured and nearly executed in 1920. It was his first of many near-death experiences.

Yeo-Thomas returned to France in the interwar years and escaped to England in 1940 after Dunkirk. Being fluent in French and English, he worked first as an interpreter before enlisting in the RAF. He was soon recruited by SOE to act as a liaison with the *Bureau Central de Renseignements et d'Action* (BCRA), de Gaulle's Free French intelligence service. He underwent full operative training and was then infiltrated into France by parachute on 25 February 1943. It was his first mission, code named *Seahorse*. Along with two French officers, Majors Pierre Brossolette and Andre Dewavrin, he worked to organise and plan strategy with the French resistance. He was able to take charge of and exfiltrate an American pilot who had been shot down, before returning to England via a clandestine Lysander pick-up. Back in England, he sought and got an audience with Churchill to convince him of the need to support the French resistance.

Yeo-Thomas was parachuted back into France on his second mission, *Marie Claire*, in September 1943 to survey the resistance groups following the capture of de Gaulle's resistance chief Jean Moulin. But in making his extensive tour of the groups he became known to the Gestapo, who called him 'The White Rabbit' for his ability to elude capture. Despite his notoriety, he continued to move freely about and on one occasion encountered Gestapo Captain Klaus Barbie, the 'Butcher of Lyon', on a train without being challenged or recognised. On no fewer than six occasions he

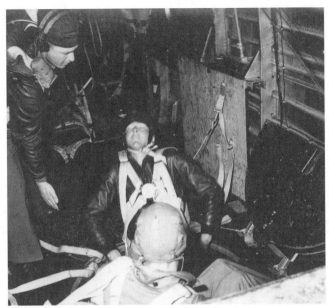

Operative departing through the 'Joe Hole' of a B-24. (492nd Bombing Group Files, US Air War College Archives)

narrowly avoided arrest. He was again exfiltrated from France by Lysander and returned to England, where he continued his work as the second-in-command of the RF section.

His third mission, *Asymtote*, was to prove Yeo-Thomas's most challenging. When Pierre Brossolette, a French SOE agent and close friend, was captured shortly after being infiltrated into the Brittany coastal region, Yeo-Thomas insisted on being reinserted to attempt a rescue. It was an extreme risk to allow his return as he knew the names and operations of all the resistance networks. On the night of 24 February 1944, he parachuted into France to make the attempt.

As it turned out, Yeo-Thomas was unable to save his friend. Brossolette died after falling or jumping to his death from the Gestapo headquarters in Paris where he was being held. Yeo-Thomas's luck would run out shortly thereafter when he was arrested after being compromised by a traitor in the network.

What followed was a remarkable story of endurance and single-minded determination that is best recounted by his George Cross citation published in *The London Gazette* on 15 February 1946:

> This officer was again parachuted into France in February 1944. Despite every security precaution, he was betrayed to the Gestapo in Paris on 21 March. While being taken by car to Gestapo Headquarters, he was badly 'beaten up'. He then underwent 4 days continuous interrogation, interspersed with beatings and torture, including immersions, head downwards, in ice-cold water, with legs and arms chained. Interrogations later continued for 2 months and Wing Commander Yeo-Thomas was offered his freedom in return for information concerning the Head of a Resistance Secretariat. Owing to his wrist being cut by chains, he contracted blood-poisoning and nearly lost his left arm. He made two daring but unsuccessful attempts to escape. He was then confined in solitude in Fresnes prison for 4 months, including 3 weeks in a darkened cell with very little food. Throughout these months of almost continuous torture, he steadfastly refused to disclose any information.
>
> On 17 July, Wing Commander Yeo-Thomas was sent with a party to Compiègne prison, from which he twice attempted to escape. He and 36 others were transferred to Buchenwald. On the way, they stopped at Saarbrücken, where they were beaten and kept in a tiny hut. They arrived at Buchenwald on 16 August and 16 of them were executed and cremated on 10 September. Wing Commander Yeo-Thomas had already commenced to organise resistance within the camp and remained undaunted by the prospect of a similar fate. He accepted an opportunity of changing his identity with that of a dead French prisoner, on condition that other officers would also be enabled to do so. In this way, he was instrumental in saving the lives of two officers.
>
> Wing Commander Yeo-Thomas was later transferred to a work kommando for Jews. In attempting to escape, he was picked up by a German patrol and, claiming French nationality, was transferred to a camp near Marienburg for French prisoners of war. On 16 April 1945, he led a party of 20 in a most gallant attempt to escape in broad daylight. Ten of them were killed by gunfire from the guards. Those who reached cover split up into small groups. Wing Commander Yeo-Thomas became separated from his companions after 3 days without food. He continued alone for a week and was recaptured when only 800 yards from the American lines. A few days later, he escaped with a party of 10 French prisoners of war, whom he led through German patrols to the American lines.
>
> Wing Commander Yeo-Thomas thus turned his final mission into a success by his determined opposition to the enemy, his strenuous efforts

to maintain the morale of his fellow prisoners and his brilliant escape activities. He endured brutal treatment and torture without flinching and showed the most amazing fortitude and devotion to duty throughout his service abroad, during which he was under the constant threat of death.

La Souris Blanche – *Captain Nancy Wake (SOE)*

One of the 'baddest' as well as one of the most decorated of SOE operatives, Nancy Wake was with the French resistance from the very beginning.

Born in New Zealand and raised in Australia, she moved to France in the 1930s as a journalist. In 1933, she travelled to Vienna to interview Hitler after the *Anschluß* of Austria. There she witnessed the Nazi oppression of the Jewish population and vowed to do whatever she could to oppose the evil of National Socialism.

She married a French industrialist, Henri Fiocca, and was living in Marseille when the war broke out. Immediately, she joined the resistance and worked as a courier for the *Maquis*. She then began to assist young men and Jews to escape across the Pyrenees into Spain. Before long she was in the cross hairs of the Gestapo, but escaped to England where she was recruited by SOE and trained as an operative. Along with another SOE officer, John Farmer, she jumped into the Auvergne region of France to coordinate resistance operations and prepare to divert German troops and prevent them from reinforcing Normandy and opposing the D-Day landings.

From all accounts, she was as hard as the men she worked with and perhaps deadlier. She used her good looks to deceive the enemy and her skills as an operative to kill them. Like Yeo-Thomas, Wake received a Gestapo nickname for her ability to evade them: the 'White Mouse'.

At the height of the D-Day invasion, she had control of around 7,000 *Maquis* that were interrupting the daily routine of a German division in the Auvergne. The attacks she led included a raid on a Gestapo headquarters in Montluçon and a firearms factory, during which she killed a sentry with her bare hands. According

Captain Nancy Wake's George Cross Medal citation

This officer was parachuted into France on 29 November 1944, as assistant to an organiser who was taking over the direction of an important circuit in Central France. The day after their arrival she and her chief found themselves stranded and without directions through the arrest of their contact, but ultimately reached their rendezvous by their own initiative. She worked for several months helping to train and instruct *Maquis* groups.

Lieutenant Wake took part in several engagements with the enemy, and showed the utmost bravery under fire. During a German attack due to the arrival by parachute of two American officers to help in the *Maquis,* she personally took command of a section of 10 men whose leader was demoralised. She led them to within point-blank range of the enemy, directed their fire, rescued the two American officers and withdrew in good order. She showed exceptional courage and coolness in the face of enemy fire.

When the *Maquis* group with which she was working was broken up by large-scale German attacks and wireless contact was lost, Lieutenant Wake went along to find a wireless operator through whom she could contact London. She covered some 200 kilometres on foot and by remarkable steadfastness and perseverance succeeded in getting a message through to London. It was largely due to these efforts that the circuit was able to start work again. Lieutenant Wake's organising ability, endurance, courage and complete disregard for her own safety earned her the respect and admiration of all. The *Maquis* troops, most of them rough and difficult to handle, accepted orders from her, and treated her as one of their own male officers.

to Wake, during that raid she confronted a German guard and despatched him with what she described as a 'karate chop' to the neck just as her instructor had taught. Up to that moment, she didn't believe it could kill – it did.

Wake was also awarded the US Medal of Freedom with Palm, the French *Chevalier de l'Ordre National de la Legion d'Honneur* and the *Officier de l'Ordre National de la Legion d'Honneur*. She also loved gin and tonics, and her last wish was for her ashes to be scattered over the mountains where she fought with the resistance.

Nancy Wake. (AWM P00885.001, Public Domain)

Eric Erickson, Swedish-American Businessman and Spy (OSS)

Wars often make for strange bedfellows, and the case of Swedish-American Eric Erickson, aka Agent Red is one of those stories.

For the OSS and SOE, Sweden's neutrality and proximity to Germany provided an extremely lucrative environment in which to operate. Its ports provided access to interview sailors, refugees and travellers who might have information on German troop and supply movements into Norway.

Although ostensibly neutral, Sweden's factories were providing Germany with precision materials such as ball bearings from the SKF *Svenska Kullagerfabriken* (Swedish Ball Bearing Factory), which represented at least 7 per cent of what its industry needed. OSS officers working out of the US Embassy were able to recruit sources that provided information on shipments, which in at least one case led to the sinking of a ship. More precise information was required, however, and an OSS SI officer recruited a source within the company that revealed the scale of the shipments. With that data, a United States Economic Warfare Mission was able to induce the Swedes to stop the trade.

Eric Erickson proved to be perhaps the most important intelligence asset that OSS would run during the war. Born in Brooklyn to emigrant parents, Erickson attended Cornell University and made millions in the Texas oilfields. In the 1930s, he made his way to Stockholm, became a Swedish citizen and decided to make even more money by providing oil to the Nazi regime (not unlike Standard Oil, which dealt with Germany until 1941).

The word soon got out and Erickson was black-listed by the US Government and disowned by his own family. Forced to face reality, in 1942 he offered his services to the OSS – or possibly he was 'asked' to help his country. Whatever happened, he was tasked to collect information on the German industrial sector, and especially its synthetic oil production. This he did with his usual panache. He spoke several languages and was socially adept, an extrovert who was able to meet SS-Chief Heinrich Himmler and convince him that he was going to build a synthetic oil facility in Sweden. Himmler gave Erickson a special pass that allowed him to visit Wintershall GmbH, Germany's largest oil producer, as well as other companies. Travelling on numerous occasions not only to collect production data but locations of the factories, he fed the information to his OSS handlers either in Stockholm or through the Swedish legation in Berlin.

Armed with the coordinates, the US Air Force and RAF were able to target and bomb many of the factories. On one occasion, 'Red' was touring a Mercedes-Benz factory when an air raid took place, forcing him to take cover with the plant employees in the company shelter.

The Germans began to suspect Erickson and made efforts to capture him, but he managed to evade them. For the remainder of the war he dealt with Japanese representatives, who believed he could help with some of their strategic supply needs.

Erickson survived the war to be honoured by US President Harry S. Truman with the Medal of Freedom.

Virginia Hall Goillot, The Limping Lady (SOE/OSS)

Virginia Hall was a unique operator in the annals of the SOE, the OSS, as well as the CIA for her activities in Europe during the war and long after.

Hall was born in Baltimore, Maryland and from the beginning was possessed with an adventurous spirit. She wanted to be a diplomat but was rejected by the U.S. Foreign Service because she was disabled – she had lost her left leg below the knee following a hunting accident in Turkey.

Despite that handicap, she served with the ambulance corps in France before it fell to the Germans in WWII, escaped through Spain to England, and then volunteered for service with the SOE. Trained in all the 'black arts' before she travelled to Spain and then France, she worked undercover as a stringer journalist for the New York Post in Lyon.

Once Germany declared war on the United States, Hall (codename 'Philomene') remained in France and went under deeper cover to provide the Allies with intelligence and assist downed pilots to escape the Germans as part of the 'Heckler' network. Working under great pressure from both the Germans and the SOE bureaucracy to safeguard her operations, she became adept as a logistician and was one of the key SOE operatives in France, supplying other agents and the resistance with money, weapons, and other supplies that were parachuted into France.

She developed another skill, arranging jailbreaks and at one point helped several SOE agents, including Georges Bégué escape from a Vichy prison into Spain.

After 14 months, and with the Germans ruthlessly dismantling the resistance's intelligence networks, she was forced to flee back to Spain, completing a grueling overland winter trek through the Pyrenees Mountains. At one point during the march she radioed London and informed them that 'Cuthbert' was giving her problems. Unaware that she was speaking of her prosthetic leg, London radioed back, 'If Cuthbert is giving you difficulty, have him eliminated.'

Following her escape, she worked undercover, again as a journalist for four months in Spain but quickly grew weary of the boring office routine and requested a transfer to the newly formed American OSS.

In March 1944, she was inserted into France via Royal Navy Motor Gunboat 502 to help prepare the way for the Normandy invasion. For the next weeks she worked as a radio operator in the Haute-Loire region. She arranged parachute drops of arms and supplies for the resistance groups and reported German troop dispositions back to headquarters. The Germans desperately sought to find her radio in order to capture what they called 'the most dangerous spy in France,' but Hall managed to elude them by staying constantly on the move.

All clandestine radio contacts had to be carried out with great care. Hall would go to a remote location to meet her radio operator (although she was a qualified operator herself). They would set up the equipment and she would quickly tap out a message in encrypted Morse code. As soon as they finished, the gear was dismantled and they would go their separate ways, never to return to the same spot twice. During the few minutes she was transmitting, the Germans would try to find her hiding site by using mobile radio direction finding trucks to triangulate her position. Anything more than five minutes on the air could mean arrest and interrogation by the Gestapo.

Just prior to the invasion, Hall along with two other OSS officers put three trained battalions of resistance fighters into action, destroying four bridges, derailing trains, and cutting a key rail link to aid the Allied advance into France from the landing beaches.

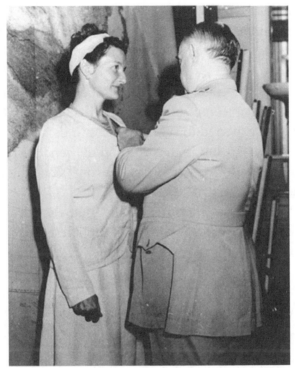

Virginia Hall being decorated by MG Donovan. (NARA)

She was honored by the British government with the Member of the Order of the British Empire. She was decorated by Major General Donovan with the Distinguished Service Cross, the United States' second highest military decoration. She was the only civilian woman to be so honored.

She married a fellow OSS officer, Paul Gaston Goillot, after the war and continued to serve the intelligence community overseas until she retired in 1966. She died at the age of 77 in July 1982.

Operation Greenup (OSS)

Greenup was the most successful of the OSS SI collection operations in Austria. This mission infiltrated two Operational Group (OG) operatives, Frederick Mayer and Hans Wijnberg, along with Franz Weber, an Austrian deserter, into the mountainous Tyrol district in late February 1945. Their task was to collect information on SS-Chief Himmler's southern *AlpenFestung* (Alpine Redoubt) headquarters, which the Allies expected to be the final defensive location for Hitler's Third Reich.

Flying out of the OSS's Italian base at Bari on a 'Carpetbagger' B-24, they were parachuted onto a glacier 10,000ft up in the mountains. The team expected to ski from there to their safe house, but two pairs of skis were lost in the drop and they ended up struggling though the waist-deep snow, while the one skier dragged their equipment behind him.

Once established at their alpine hideout, the team began to collect intelligence from friendly locals and a resistance unit of the Provisional Austrian National Committee (POEN). The team was able to send location details on two aircraft factories at Jenbach and Kematen, as well as on the *AlpenFestung*. They sent the information back by W/T, enabling air raids on the facilities. It soon became clear to Mayer that the *AlpenFestung* was a ruse and he began to report that the existing intelligence was wrong. However, the Allied high command refused to discount the information, and would eventually send the US Seventh Army across southern Germany to ensure that the redoubt was captured.

Nevertheless, Mayer's team established that the Germans were planning rail movements through the Brenner Pass around the US Fifteenth Air Force's regularly scheduled bombing raids. With that information, air planners began to vary the raids' timing and managed to catch several trains in the pass and block it completely.

Mayer was a German Jewish émigré who moved to the United States before the war. When Pearl Harbor was attacked he volunteered for the US Army, but was refused because of his nationality – he was considered an 'enemy alien'. Able to speak German, French and Spanish, as well as English, the OSS realised his potential and snatched him up to be trained as an OG operative. Now deep in the Tyrol, he decided on a more audacious mission, travelling to Innsbruck to collect information on the German military there.

Team GREENUP in Austria following their successful mission: Franz Weber, Hans Wijnberg and Frederick Mayer. (US Army Photo, NARA)

With documentation identifying him as a wounded officer, he wore a German uniform into the city and even found accommodation at the German barracks, where he was able to gather details on movement timetables and troop strengths in the area.

After three months, he changed his cover to that of a Frenchman escaping the Soviet advance in the East, but his cover was blown by a black marketeer who had been arrested by the Gestapo. The criminal betrayed Mayer as an American agent, and he too was arrested. Mayer underwent days of torture but maintained his story of working alone. Ironically, an American agent, Hermann Matull, of OSS Team DEADWOOD, had also been captured and was undergoing interrogation nearby. He was shown Mayer's photograph and asked if he could identify him. Matull cleverly insisted that

Mayer was an important American officer and should only be interrogated by the regional political leader, *Gauleiter* Franz Hofer. He lied even more to say that if Mayer was harmed there would be negative consequences. By this time in the war, the Germans were worried about the approach of the Russian Army and Hofer was looking to find an escape route.

Hofer ordered Mayer to be brought to him and invited him to dinner. Mayer initially thought he was being tricked into revealing where his teammates were, but came to realise that Hofer wanted to surrender to the Americans. Mayer was able to send a message to the OSS headquarters in Bern, Switzerland, through another German officer. The OSS Bern office was under the command of Allen Dulles, future chief of the CIA, who forwarded the message on to Bari.

On 3 May 1945, Mayer and a German escort were driven out to meet the approaching American 103rd Infantry Division. With his car flying a white bed sheet of surrender, Mayer jumped out of the car to present himself to the American column and tell them Innsbruck was an open city, which led to the peaceful surrender of the city and ultimately the whole Tyrol region.

In total, the OSS infiltrated 12 OG/SI teams into Austria, five of which successfully transmitted intelligence to headquarters. Mayer would later be known as the real 'Inglorious Bastard'. Nominated for the Medal of Honor, he was eventually awarded the Legion of Merit.

Creating General Mayhem

Kidnapping the General: the Kreipe Operation (SOE)

The story of the resistance on the Greek island of Crete reads like a story from Hellenic mythology. It is full of tragic, flawed warriors who struggled valiantly against a terrible foe.

When the island fell to a German invasion in 1941, many of the 400,000 inhabitants banded together immediately to oppose the Nazi occupation. In May 1941, the Patriotic Front of Crete (PMK) was organised as a communist group. It later took the name of the mainland communist National Liberation Front (EAM).

A second group, the Supreme Committee of Cretan Struggle (AEAK), was formed two weeks after the fall of Crete. It became the National Organization of Crete (EOK) in 1943. It was intended to act as a counterweight to the EAM, with the help of SOE's Force 133. Unlike the resistance groups of the mainland, on Crete EAM and EOK resolved to work together and avoided much of the internecine struggle that later took place. Guerrillas were known collectively as the *Andartes*.

John Pendlebury was the first English name to be entered into the Pantheon of heroes on Crete. He would be joined by many Greeks. Pendlebury was a member of the British Army contingent on the island when the Germans invaded – an archaeologist, linguist and now British intelligence officer, he knew the island as well as most of its natives. As the rest of the British evacuated the island, he resolved to stay on and fight with the guerrillas and he withdrew to the Nidha plateau on Mount Ida with his friend and fellow brigand, Kapetan Satanas.

As the Germans advanced across the island, Pendlebury and Satanas tried to launch attacks on the German flank to slow their advance, but Pendlebury was wounded and captured in civilian clothing by the Germans. Accused of being a spy, he was summarily shot. Unfortunately for the Germans, his spirit animated the Greeks as much as the loss of one of their own. During the final evacuation of the last of the British forces, Satanas persuaded the commander to leave their weapons behind, telling him: 'We will carry on the fight till you return.'

Directly after the British left Crete, Christopher 'Monty' Woodhouse was sent in to organise SOE's operations on Crete. He recruited George J. Doundoulakis, a Greek-American who had been working at the British headquarters on Crete as a translator before the German invasion, to assist him. Woodhouse was replaced by Thomas James 'Yanni' Dunbabin, and under his command Doundoulakis expanded his intelligence network that assisted SOE to track German shipping in the Mediterranean as well as monitor their activities on the island.

'Yanni' was joined by 'Paddy' Leigh Fermor in 1942. Like those who preceded him, Fermor was an adventurer as well as an accomplished author and linguist. He had been commissioned on the 'General List' as an intelligence officer and assigned as a liaison officer to the Greek army in Albania, and was evacuated from Crete when it fell. Around 30,000 German soldiers and a 10,000-man Italian contingent turned the island into *Festung Kreta* (Fortress Crete). Invasion fears would periodically swell the occupation forces to nearly 75,000 men.

When he returned to Crete, Fermor took charge of guerrilla activities on the western part of the island. In September 1943, when Italy signed the armistice with the Allies, Fermor made contact with the commander of the 30,000-strong Italian garrison in the eastern part of the island, General Angelico Carta. Carta, knowing the Germans who held the western part of Crete would punish the Italians, decided to abandon his post along with his staff and sought Fermor's help to escape.

Fermor radioed SOM Cairo and arranged for a Motor Torpedo Boat (MTB) to pick up Carta and his staff off the south-eastern coast of Crete. As Carta was about to be whisked away to Egypt, Fermor found himself unable to return to the shore because of rough surf and had to remain on the boat. In Cairo, with the Carta evacuation as proof of the concept, Fermor was able to discuss another operation that had already been under consideration – the abduction of the German commander on the island.

Dunbabin and another SOE officer, Xan Fielding, had begun planning for such an event, first targetting German *Generalmajor* Alexander Andrae and then, when he was posted elsewhere, Bruno Bräer. By the time Fermor posited the plan to SOM in Cairo, *Generalmajor* Friedrich-Wilhelm Müller was in charge. Müller was a most disagreeable person. Known as the 'Butcher of Crete' for atrocities he had ordered, even the most reluctant of the British commanders leaned towards approving the plan. Several did not, fearing reprisals, but planning went ahead.

Fermor was to be parachuted back into Crete along with his colleague, William ('Billy') Stanley Moss, and two Cretan-Greeks, George Tirakis and Manoli Paterakis. Over Crete, however, only Fermor was able to exit the airplane before cloud cover prevented the others from jumping. The three returned to base and would try 12 times before the air route was abandoned and they went by sea – arriving two months later in April 1944.

By that time, Müller had been replaced by another officer, Heinrich Kreipe, who became the new target. The team had already decided that the best place to abduct the general was on the road between his headquarters outside Heraklion and his home, Villa Ariadni, several kilometres away. After the beach landing, the team made its way across the island on foot, supported and hidden by the *Andartes* and the local underground.

Their ambush point was set up a kilometre down the road from the German HQ at Ano Archanes (see diagram). On 26 April, Billy Moss and Paddy Fermor arrived at the site dressed in German uniforms, with another five resistance members backing them up. At the approach of Kreipe's car, they signalled for it to stop and pulled the driver out. With the general restrained in the back of the car, Fermor impersonated Kreipe while Moss drove. They went through Heraklion, passing 22 checkpoints before abandoning the vehicle west of the city and splitting up.

Moss initially moved south into the mountains with the general up towards Psiloritis, where he reunited with Fermor and the rest of the team. They then climbed over Mount Ida while playing cat and mouse with a huge German search team that cut them off from their original exfiltration point of Saktouria and required them to divert far to the west. The *Andartes* who took the driver hostage grew tired of his inability to keep up and shot him.

Making contact with several dispersed SOE operatives who were working with the guerrillas along the way, Fermor was able to radio for a new pickup point at Rodakino. Finally, on the night of 14 May and after a marathon overland trek of 154km, the team was picked

Kreipe Abduction Team (left to right): Georgios Tyrakis, William Stanley Moss, Patrick Leigh Fermor, Emmanouil Paterakis, Antonios Papaleonidas. (Gabrielle Bullock/Wikimedia CC)

up by SBS boats and evacuated to Mersa Matruh in Egypt. There was one last complication when neither Moss nor Fermor knew the Morse code for the pickup signal. Luckily, another SOE officer who was travelling back to Egypt with them, Dennis Ciclitira (aka 'Dionysis'), took the torch and made the signal, calling his colleagues 'bloody fools'.

Much to Fermor's dismay, the raid did have repercussions. Despite efforts to make the abduction look like a purely British affair, the Germans sent Müller back to Crete to take revenge. In mid-August, Müller took little account of the British attempt at deception and ordered the town of Anogeia, a centre for the resistance on the island, to be destroyed, along with Damasta, a village near the site of another partisan ambush that killed 30 German soldiers on 7 August 1944. As a result, over 50 men and

The route followed by the Kreipe abduction team from landing to exfiltration. (Map: James Stejskal)

women were executed, 900 homes were destroyed and around 1,500 villagers displaced.

In May 1945, Dennis Ciclitira met with the then commander, *Generalmajor* Hans-Georg Benthack, to arrange the German surrender on the island. Because Benthack was required to surrender to an officer of equal rank, Ciclitira needed to contact the British HQ, which he did in a manner of minutes. When the German wanted to know how Ciclitira was able to accomplish that feat so quickly, Ciclitira responded that his radio was hidden only three doors away, where its transmissions had been masked by the Germans' own radio traffic.

It was no surprise the occupiers wondered whether it was the Germans or the British who controlled Crete. The Cretan resistance, with SOE's assistance and support, was one of the most tenacious of the war. Over 20,000 men and women died during the occupation of Crete, from its capture on 20 May 1941 until its liberation on 15 May 1945.

Paddy Fermor was decorated with a Distinguished Service Order and Billy Moss won a Military Cross for the action to capture *Generalmajor* Kreipe.

Creek Force: the Last Charge of the Calcutta Light Horse (SOE)

Occasionally, SOE had to make do with the best available resources. Such was the case with Creek Force.

In 1939, four Axis merchant ships – three German (the *Ehrenfels*, *Drachenfels* and *Braunfels*) and one Italian (the *Anfora*) – sought refuge at Marmagoa in Portuguese Goa on the south-western coast of India. They were seeking the safety of a neutral port. At first, the British thought they were of little concern but, as time passed, they began to suspect the crews were transmitting information on Allied shipping, including cargoes and destinations. The biggest clue was a spike in sinkings; 46 Allied merchant ships were sunk over six weeks, then another 12 in early March 1943.

British intelligence in India confirmed that the *Ehrenfels* was using a radio to send information, despite the fact that its primary communication system had been removed. Apparently, it had a second high-powered set aboard that the Portuguese had either overlooked or ignored – perhaps in return for a bribe.

The British protested the transgression as the Germans were ignoring maritime neutrality laws. When nothing happened and the transmissions continued, alternative courses of action were tried. The first was to abduct the German intelligence chief in Goa, Robert Koch, code name 'Trompeta'. When the transmissions resumed, another tack was chosen.

Lieutenant Colonel Lewis Pugh, SOE's Director of Country Sections in Calcutta, had an idea. He suggested a raiding party might be able to take care of the problem, boarding the ships and putting the radio out of action. Because Marmagoa was a neutral port, official British military action would not be possible. The raid would have to be completely clandestine and disavowable. He had in mind an outfit that could pull it off: the Calcutta Light Horse (CLH), a semi-reserve cavalry unit, semi-social club of former military men who were mostly too old for the war, but not too old to be put completely out to pasture. Pugh was also a member of the CLH and met Colonel William 'Bill' Grice, the unit's commander, to propose the operation to him. Grice, happy to play a part in the mission, brought together the other men to see who else might volunteer. As might be expected, to a man they all did. Only 14 of the 30 or so present were up to the ardours of the task, however, as it would involve a 1,200-mile train ride across India and then a 'short' 300-mile boat trip to the target. Because Pugh needed 18 men, four more volunteers came from another outfit: the Calcutta Scottish, another British volunteer regiment-cum-social club. Pugh named the group Creek Force; the operation was codenamed *Longshanks*.

With recruitment completed, a short training course was conducted to refamiliarise the men with the profession of arms. One can imagine it was probably not too strenuous, so as not to lose any of the volunteers before the fighting began.

The operation's raiding boat, *Phoebe*, a 209ft river barge piloted by retired Royal Navy Commander Bernard Davis, departed Calcutta and sailed along the eastern coast of India, around the southernmost tip to the port of Cochin after a stop at Trincomalee, Ceylon, to refuel. At the same time, the force travelled by train from Calcutta through Madras to Cochin in small groups to avoid looking like a band of over-the-hill mercenaries. One last cog in the wheel was Trooper Jock Cartwright, who was sent into Portuguese Goa to make the advance arrangements for the 'festivities'. And there would be festivities…

Pugh gave Cartwright ample funds to co-opt most of the bar and brothel keepers in Marmagoa and set up a huge party for all the seamen on the evening of the raid. It was hoped that the prospect of free beer and 'entertainment' would draw the crews off the ships and into the city.

To the south in Cochin, the team rendezvoused with *Phoebe* and, once onboard, continued their way slowly up the coast. The men, who were armed only with pistols for the train journey, then received the equipment that Pugh arranged for the mission. While Sten guns, grenades and explosives were available in plenty, Grice dictated that no shooting was to take place. He did not want any dead Germans to detract from the mission's purpose of silencing the radio.

The plan was to divide the team into three task groups: one to seize the ship's bridge, one to find the radio and another to cut the anchor chain.

On the night of 9 March 1943, *Phoebe*, running with no lights, came into the harbour and headed straight for the *Ehrenfels*. As the barge came alongside, grappling hooks and ladders went up against the German ship's hull and the boarding party raced onto the freighter. There was little opposition, but a burst of gunfire alerted the few crew remaining on the ship. One of the crew dropped an incendiary device onto the codebooks, while his mates did their best to slow the assault. *Kapitän* Roefer and eight of his crew were killed in the ensuing melee. The radio was found below decks, in a locked compartment, and destroyed before the seacocks were opened and the ship began to list.

Grice, realising there was little time to lose, told Davis to sound the withdrawal signal with three blasts from the barge's horn. The assault force clambered back over the side of the stricken ship, which was sinking while burning fiercely from the explosives and incendiary charges set by both sides.

The few sailors of the other ships, fully expecting to be boarded, decided that discretion was the better part of valour and chose to scuttle their vessels. The harbour was soon brightly lit by the ships' funeral pyres.

Phoebe, its crew safely back on board, turned out to sea and disappeared into the night, its Jolly Roger fluttering in the night air.

There were no medal parades or official announcements of the deed. HMG chose instead to promulgate the story that the crews of the ships had clashed over politics and rebelled. Only in 1978, when James Leasor wrote a book, *The Boarding Party*, and told the story did the mission became known to the general public.

The foreword written by the Earl Mountbatten of Burma states, 'This book tells how fourteen of them [the CLH], with four colleagues from the Calcutta Scottish, another Auxiliary Force unit, volunteered for a hazardous task which, for reasons the author makes plain, no-one else was able to undertake. This happened shortly before my arrival in India in 1943, as Supreme Allied Commander, South East Asia, and immediately [I] saw how valuable were the results of this secret operation. I am pleased that at last credit may be given to those who planned and carried it out.'

Strategic Sabotage and Destruction

Operation Anthropoid *(SOE)*

Time: 10:35am. Date: 27 May 1942. Location: Prague.

A Czech paratrooper, Josef Gabčík, steps into the street as an official German Mercedes Benz 320C with the license plate 'SS 3' slows down for a sharp curve in Holešovickách Street. The vehicle is carrying *SS Obergruppenführer* Reinhard Heydrich, the German Reich Protector of the occupied Czech provinces of Bohemia and Moravia. Known as the 'Blond Beast' by his colleagues, he personally represents all that is evil in the Nazis. In the next seconds, the fate of thousands of Czech citizens would be sealed. Jan Kubiš, Gabčík's partner, covers him a few metres away, while Josef Valčík, 100 metres further up the road, acts as spotter.

The car approaches and Gabčík swings his Sten into firing position and pulls the trigger. The weapon jams. Kubiš, seeing his partner's difficulty, lobs a grenade modified with an impact fuse at the car as Heydrich stands up to shoot at his attackers. The grenade strikes the car just behind the passenger seat and explodes, driving metal shrapnel and cloth fragments into the interior of the car, many of which wound Heydrich.

Heydrich stumbles from the car, fires his pistol at Kubiš, and then collapses. His driver, SS-*Oberscharführer* Johannes Klein, gives chase and is wounded twice by Gabčík's Colt M1903. A passing woman recognises Heydrich and summons a passing delivery truck to transport Heydrich to a hospital. In the meantime, Gabčík and

Reinhard Heydrich's damaged Mercedes in Prague after the attack. (Bundesarchiv Bild 146-1972-039-44)

Kubiš escape without ensuring Heydrich is dead. Heydrich does not appear badly injured, but his immune system cannot cope with the foreign material introduced into his body by the blast. He develops septicaemia and dies a week later.

This was one of the most controversial SOE operations of World War II. Initiated by the Czech government in exile with the assistance of the British, it unleashed a whirlwind of retribution by the German occupiers.

Following the attack, Deputy Reich Protector *SS Gruppenführer* Karl Hermann Frank and SS-Chief Heinrich Himmler in Berlin decided on retribution. Within days of the attack, the Czech population began to feel the wrath of the SS. The Germans killed an estimated 5,000 Czechs, at least 3,000 of them Jews, to avenge their comrade.

Heydrich was named Acting Reich Protector to Bohemia and Moravia in September 1941 when his predecessor, Konstantin von Neurath, was unable to quell civilian strikes against the Nazi occupation. Germany needed the protectorate's industrial capacity to feed its war-machine. Hitler decided Neurath needed to be replaced and Heydrich was selected to bring order to the troubled region.

Heydrich was already well known for his barbarity. He started with the notorious *Schutzstaffel* (SS), and by 1939 headed the Reich Main Security Office (the RHSA). In this position he was responsible for the suppression of any opposition to the Hitler regime throughout Germany and the occupied territories. He created the Operational Groups (*Einsatzgruppen*) which systematically eliminated around a million people – partisans as well as civilians – in Eastern Europe.

As soon as Heydrich moved into Prague's Czernin Palace, he immediately declared martial law and executed 300 members of the opposition and intelligentsia. Heydrich began the transport of Jews from the Protectorate to concentration camps and established a Jewish ghetto in the ancient Bohemian town of Terezín (known as Theresienstadt to the Germans), where at least 35,000 Jews would die.

The Czech population's demonstrations were quickly quelled. Heydrich penetrated the Czech underground and eliminated the majority of its leadership. Most Czech military fighters had left the country, going to France to fight openly at the side of the French and British before being evacuated to Britain, where they formed the nucleus of the Czech Army-in-exile.

To that point, the Czech resistance had been principally concerned with gathering intelligence, not direct action against the Germans. Many felt that any armed confrontation would lead to retribution, something they wished to avoid. Perhaps worse, the government in the occupied territory failed to repudiate the Munich Agreement and even cooperated with the Nazis.

This was a serious problem for Czech President-in-exile Edvard Beneš, who sought support from France and Britain in anticipation of his eventual return to power in his homeland.

His main difficulty lay in the failure of Britain and France to renounce the 1938 Munich conference that permitted Germany to annex Bohemia and Moravia – the so-called German *Sudetenland* – in the first place. As long as that was the case, the exiled Czech government felt that the country would not be allowed return to its pre-agreement borders after the war.

Beneš thought that a spectacular action like the assassination of a senior German would swing the Allies to repudiate the Munich Agreement and provide more support for the resistance movement.

With his Chief of Intelligence, Colonel František Moravec, Beneš decided to engage the British SOE to determine a potential target. His hope was that this show of action would demonstrate his people's resistance to German occupation, possibly influence the war and cement his role as leader of the Czech people.

Heydrich ultimately became the logical choice. There is ample evidence that the British leadership, certainly Prime Minister Winston Churchill, was fully apprised of Beneš's intent and the target of the mission, dubbed Operation *Anthropoid*.

With SOE assistance, two Czech warrant officers, Josef Gabčík and Jan Kubiš, were assessed, selected and trained for the mission. Kubiš was actually a second choice, replacing Staff Sergeant Karel Svoboda, who was injured in a parachute-training jump. Gabčík and Kubiš were first trained as parachutists, then sent to STS 25 to receive paramilitary training. The assessment process was rigorous, and a number of candidates were observed and interviewed.

The men were told only that they were being considered for a special mission and were asked to volunteer. Those who did were observed in normal training for traits that would serve them as a clandestine operator. Foremost among these was discipline in the area of operational security.

Once the candidate group was reduced to six, a unique method was used to narrow it even further. Each candidate was given a different snippet of information and warned not to divulge it to anyone. The testers then waited for rumours to pop up in the training camp. When two of the stories became common knowledge, the candidates who had been entrusted with the specific details were easily eliminated from the programme.

Gabčík and Kubiš were parachuted from a modified Handley-Page Halifax bomber into a drop zone about 40km from Prague during the early hours of 29 December 1941. They made contact with members of the resistance who were to give them assistance for the mission. Fortuitously, none of them had been compromised to the Germans. They then proceeded to Prague, where they began to prepare for the mission.

Little is known of Gabčík and Kubiš's activities from January until the attack. It is known that they stayed with relatives and members of the resistance, and made contact with teams of Czech special operators who had also been parachuted into the country for other missions. They also developed at least two other plans for killing Heydrich, including an ambush outside Prague and an attempt on a train. Both were scrubbed in favour of the V Holešovickách Street site.

On 27 May 1942, Gabčík and Kubiš made their move. As related above, Heydrich's wounds from the grenade blast would prove fatal. With this act, the fate of thousands of Czechs was sealed. When the news reached Hitler, he instructed SS *Reichsführer* Himmler that the SS should 'wade in blood' to avenge Heydrich. This they did.

But the assassins were not found immediately. Himmler assigned SS *Obergruppenführer* Kurt Daluege to replace Heydrich and extact revenge.

On 9 June, based on erroneous information about the origin of the assassins, the SS surrounded the village of Lidice; all the men were executed and the women and children sent to concentration camps. The buildings were all burned and the remnants ploughed into the earth. The killers were still not turned in.

At end of June, Karel Čurda, a paratrooper from one of the other teams who knew the location of the *Anthropoid* team, succumbed to his fears and turned himself in to the Gestapo. Using Čurda's information, the Germans were able to locate the team along with five other resistance fighters in the crypts of the Church of St Cyril and Methodius in central Prague. The church was surrounded and a gunfight ensued that only ended with the suicide deaths of the

Czech resistance fighters. (Čurda was executed for treason following the end of the war.)

After the war, Daluege admitted at the Nurnberg Tribunals that 1,331 Czechs, 201 of them women, had been executed in reprisal, along with 3,000 prisoners from Terezin concentration camp.

The assassination was meant to be a call to arms for the population of the occupied territories. As Winston Churchill commented, 'The only way to mobilise popular support for secret armies of resistance fighters during the war was to stage such dramatic acts of terrorism against the German occupying forces.' In this regard, the mission was a failure, as the SS and the Gestapo had already crippled what was left of the resistance. The Czech underground would not pose a substantial threat to German occupation for the remainder of the war. Czech intelligence chief Colonel Moravec concluded:

> Perhaps 5,000 Czechs paid with their lives for the death of a single Nazi maniac. The cost and the worth of the killing of Heydrich has been the subject of much controversy. It is certainly true that the price paid for Heydrich was much higher than the figures indicate, for the Nazis executed systematically the very best of the nation. On the other hand, it is quite clear that had Heydrich lived he would have done no less. The eradication of the Czechoslovak nation and its amalgamation into the Reich, including the systematic murder of its leaders, was the assignment with which he came to Prague. In my opinion, the problem of cost can be reduced to a simple principle, so well understood by the parachutists Kubiš and Gabčík: freedom and, above all, liberation from slavery have to be fought for, and this means losses in human lives.

The cold, simple fact is that the assassination of Heydrich served a purpose. Beneš had resigned as President of Czechoslovakia on 5 October 1938 after the Munich Agreement was reached. His efforts in London as head of the government-in-exile were oriented on one overarching goal: renunciation of the agreement and restoration of Czechoslovakia to its pre-war state following the defeat of Germany.

On 5 August 1942, Britain revoked the Munich Agreement. Two months later, the Free French followed suit. Overall, the end effect was in concert with Gubbin's edict that 'irregular warfare served the strategic aims of the Allied leaders'.

The goal of Operation *Anthropoid* was nothing less than the repudiation of the Munich Agreement. At a terrible cost, Warrant Officers Gabčík and Kubiš accomplished their mission.

To Stop the Bomb: GROUSE, Freshman and GUNNERSIDE (SOE)

Of all the strategic sabotage operations conducted during World War II, the destruction of the Vemork Hydroelectric Plant at Rjukan in Norway ranks above all the rest.

German research into nuclear weapons began early in 1938 and came to the notice of British and American intelligence through their scientific communities. One specific aspect of the German programme, a requirement for large quantities of heavy water (D_2O) to produce the plutonium required for a weapon, made Vemork a target. It was the only facility in Europe capable of producing the heavy water the Germans needed and had come under Nazi control when Norway was invaded and occupied in 1940. The German code name for heavy water was SH-200.

In 1942, Churchill tasked the War Cabinet to deal with the problem and they decided to destroy the production facility. The task was given to the Chief of Combined Operations, Louis Mountbatten, and several options were considered:

1) internal sabotage by employees recruited for the job;
2) infiltration of the plant by a Norwegian SOE team;
3) destruction of the water intake pipeline by a larger SOE team;
4) a Combined Operations raid by 25 to 50 men; and
5) an RAF bombing raid.

Einar Skinnarland, a Norwegian who had escaped to England and been recruited but given only minimal training by SOE, was parachuted back into Norway near Lake Møs on 28 March. His mission was to get back to Rjukan and supply intelligence on the

Norsk Hydroelectric Plant, Vemork, Rjukan, Norway. (Pierce Reid)

plant. SOE had another man, Jomar Brun, inside the plant already. Separately, they would provide detailed intelligence on the workings and security of the plant and the surrounding area.

Whichever option was chosen, the head of *Kompani Linge*, the Norwegian SOE contingent, wanted his people on the ground to prepare the way. A four-man Norwegian team had already been trained for the contingency: team commander Jens-Anton Poulsson, Arne Kjelstrup, radio operator Knut Haugland and Claus Helberg. Called Team GROUSE, they were infiltrated onto the Hardangervidda, an inhospitable arctic mountain plateau to the north-west of Rjukan, on 18 October 1942. The decision had been made; GROUSE would prepare the way for a British Army raid, Operation *Freshman*.

The *Freshman* plan was to conduct a glider assault landing near the target and then raid the plant. The force was made up of 34 sappers from the 1st Airborne Division, trained to recognise and destroy the key components of the heavy water production process. But, the *Freshman* mission would tragically end in the skies over Norway.

On the evening of 19 November, the force started out from RAF Skitten in northern Scotland, two Horsa gliders towed by Halifax bombers. They arrived over the landing zone but could not contact the GROUSE team that was waiting because their Eureka receiver on board the aircraft had failed. Unable to find the zone, they turned to return home.

Deteriorating weather started to cause problems as the aircraft began to ice up. The towing cable of one Horsa snapped and the glider crashed into the mountains. The second Halifax released its glider before it too crashed into the mountains in poor visibility, killing the entire crew. Its glider also crashed. Most of the troops from both gliders were killed, but a number survived only to be later executed under Hitler's infamous so-called 'Commando Order', issued in October 1942 following the killing of captured German soldiers in a commando raid on Sark in the Channel Islands. In the wreckage of the gliders, German searchers found a marked map that showed Vemork as the commandos' target, which resulted in the plant's defences being strengthened considerably.

An alternative plan was needed and SOE took charge of the mission. Back in England, another six-man-strong team of Norwegians drawn from *Kompani Linge* was preparing for action: team leader Joachim Rønneberg, Kasper Idland, Frederik Kayser, Knut Haukelid, Hans Storhaug and Birger Stromsheim, the oldest at 31. Much like Team GROUSE, the six knew the area and had lived on skis for most of their lives. Their code name was GUNNERSIDE.

In Norway, Team GROUSE quickly learned of the disaster and went to ground, hiding in a small hunting cabin on the hostile plateau where few Germans dared venture. Conditions were rough, even for men accustomed to the cold winters. The team – renamed SWALLOW at headquarters – had little food. They had lost contact with their one local asset because of a German crackdown on the community. The Gestapo, looking for anyone who might have

Hitler's 'Commando Order'

The Fuhrer   SECRET
18.10.1942

1. For a long time now our opponents have been employing in their conduct of the war, methods which contravene the International Convention of Geneva. The members of the so-called Commandos behave in a particularly brutal and underhand manner; and it has been established that those units recruit criminals not only from their own country but even former convicts set free in enemy territories. From captured orders it emerges that they are instructed not only to tie up prisoners, but also to kill out-of-hand unarmed captives who they think might prove an encumbrance to them, or hinder them in successfully carrying out their aims. Orders have indeed been found in which the killing of prisoners has positively been demanded of them.

2. In this connection it has already been notified in an Appendix to Army Orders of 7.10.1942 that in future, Germany will adopt the same methods against these Sabotage units of the British and their Allies; i.e. that, whenever they appear, they shall be ruthlessly destroyed by the German troops.

3. I order, therefore:
From now on all men operating against German troops in so-called Commando raids in Europe or in Africa, are to be annihilated to the last man. This is to be carried out whether they be soldiers in uniform, or saboteurs, with or without arms; and whether fighting or seeking to escape; and it is equally immaterial whether they come into action from Ships and Aircraft, or whether they land by parachute. Even if these individuals on discovery

make obvious their intention of giving themselves up as prisoners, no pardon is on any account to be given. On this matter a report is to be made on each case to Headquarters for the information of Higher Command.

4. Should individual members of these Commandos, such as agents, saboteurs, etc., fall into the hands of the Armed Forces through any means – as, for example, through the Police in one of the Occupied Territories – they are to be instantly handed over to the SD. To hold them in military custody – for example in POW Camps, etc., even if only as a temporary measure, is strictly forbidden.

5. This order does not apply to the treatment of those enemy soldiers who are taken prisoner or give themselves up in open battle, in the course of normal operations, large scale attacks; or in major assault landings or airborne operations. Neither does it apply to those who fall into our hands after a sea fight, nor to those enemy soldiers who, after air battle, seek to save their lives by parachute.

6. I will hold all Commanders and Officers responsible under Military Law for any omission to carry out this order, whether by failure in their duty to instruct their units accordingly, or if they themselves act contrary to it.

A Hitler

HEADQUARTERS OF THE ARMY   SECRET

The enclosed Order from the Fuhrer is forwarded in connection with destruction of enemy terror and sabotage troops.

This order is intended for Commanders only and is in no circumstances to fall into Enemy hands.

Further distribution by receiving Headquarters is to be most strictly limited.

The Headquarters mentioned in the Distribution list are responsible that all parts of the Order, or extracts taken from it, which are issued are again withdrawn and, together with this copy, destroyed.

Chief of Staff of the Army
JODL

assisted the British commandos in the villages, increased their patrols in the countryside. Nevertheless, the team kept in radio contact with London. They were informed that a new team would attempt the sabotage and were told to sit and wait. It would be a long, cold two-and-a-half months of waiting, surviving off the little food that could be found.

On 16 February 1943, GUNNERSIDE parachuted into Norway. They landed far off course, some 50km away from the reception team, and it took the two teams a week to rendezvous. The GROUSE Team was happy to exchange news and get some different food.

The combined team began to plan the assault of the plant. There were several possibilities: approach the site across a deep gorge and cross over a foot bridge; climb down the hill behind the factory alongside the water intake penstocks; or descend into the gorge, cross the river at the bottom and climb back up the opposite side. From reconnaissance trips, the team knew the bridge was guarded and the ground around the penstocks was mined. That left the gorge.

On 27 February, the night of the raid, the team radio operator and a local contact were left at the hideaway cabin while the rest skied off on the mission. Nine raiders dressed in British uniforms approached the target along a sparsely travelled ridge road and descended into the steep 600ft gorge to the river. The river was low and iced over, and the team was able to cross without a problem before beginning the long, brutal climb up to the plant. They intersected an unguarded railway line that led up to the plant and walked its length to a chainlink fence that circled the factory. The Germans, apparently believing the gorge was too formidable an obstacle, left the approach open. Rønneberg had the foresight to acquire bolt cutters in England and used them to cut the fence. The obstacle breached, the men entered and split into two groups: a demolitions party of three men and the remainder as security to cover the German guardhouse and the entrance to the factory to protect the sabotage team.

The saboteurs had difficulty getting into the building. While looking for a cable tunnel, they split up. Two of the team found an alternative: an unlocked entrance. The others joined them after a short delay. With the exception of a Norwegian worker, there was no one else in the plant. The demolition team headed into the heavy water production facility, which was located deep underground, and placed the charges with short fuses to ensure they would not be cut if the team was discovered. With all in place, the team leader lit the fuses and the raiders escaped.

Thirty seconds later, the charges went off – a muffled explosion that destroyed the processing machinery but did not damage the building. Only a few windows broke and the German guards didn't react for several minutes. The team was able to escape well ahead of any Germans, got back across the gorge and disappeared, first skiing towards the town of Rjukan and then up onto the plateau.

Far away from the plant, the team split up. Five men, still in British uniform, skied for neutral Sweden 400km away, while the others headed into the countryside or to Oslo to help the local resistance.

The production of heavy water was interrupted for several months by the raid and the on-site stock of around 600kg of SH-200 was destroyed. But the plant was rebuilt and production began again in April, resulting in a decision by the Allies (without input from the Norwegian leadership in exile) to bomb the plant. From May until November, raids were carried out that damaged the plant and killed many civilians but left the repaired SH-200 plant undamaged.

The Germans finally saw the futility of trying to run the Vemork plant and decided to transfer what heavy water there was to Germany in barrels. The route would be by rail from the plant to the coast for transhipment to Germany. There was one vulnerable point where the barrels could be intercepted. After the train left Rjukan, the railcars would be put onto a ferry to cross Tinnsjå (Lake Tinn) for the onward journey. Sinking the ferry would put the barrels into the deep lake, where they could not be recovered. The only drawback was that some Norwegians would be killed in the attack, but after reconfirming orders, the go-ahead was given.

Knut Haukelid, one of the remaining GUNNERSIDE operatives, led the action. Leading a group of seven resistance members, he gained access to the quay and boarded the ferry *Hydro* while another man distracted the guards. He planted explosive charges with clockwork timers on the forward section of the keel. The train cars were loaded and the *Hydro* departed on time. Just as the ferry reached the deepest part of the lake, the charges exploded. As expected, the resulting flooding in the bow of the ship caused the rudder and screws to lift out of the water and left the ferry unable to make its way to landfall, where the cargo could be recovered. It sank with the loss of 18 lives: four Germans and 14 Norwegians.

The successful sinking of *Hydro* ended all Norwegian participation in the German nuclear programme. M. R. D. Foot heralded the operation a 'coup ... so important that nothing else the section did bears record beside it'.

Cutting the Lines: Operation Harling (SOE)

In 1942, General Harold Alexander needed some help. The battle for North Africa was beginning to tip back in favour of Britain and its allies, and he was about to launch an attack on El Alamein – the second offensive against the location. Alexander requested that measures be taken to interrupt the German supply lines that were keeping Erwin Rommel's *Afrika Korps* equipped, fuelled and fed.

The *Hydro* ferry docked on Lake Tinn before World War II. (Anders Wilse & Norwegian Museum of Cultural History; PDNorway 50)

British Headquarters in Cairo turned to the SOE. Intelligence had it that the Germans were sending supplies by rail from Germany through the Balkans to Piraeus on the Greek coast. The supplies were then transshipped across the Mediterranean to North Africa. If the rail route could be interdicted, Rommel's pipeline would run dry.

The British sent a signal to one of its sources in Greece, a network known as Prometheus II, and asked if any of three viaducts were viable targets. These were the Papadia, Asopos and Gorgopotamos viaducts – all relatively close together and situated in difficult terrain over deep gorges. Importantly, they lay on the key Salonica–Piraeus rail line.

Prometheus II responded that they were vulnerable and guarded by low-quality Italian units rather than German troops. SOE decided to send in a team to destroy one of the bridges, but would leave the final choice to the SOE team leader once on the ground. The order specified the demolition needed to take place in 30 days. Operation *Harling* was born.

In the meantime, there was one significant problem in that the British were not completely sure of the capabilities or political affiliations of the local resistance forces. There were two groups in the area. One was led by Napoleon Zervas, the founder of the republican National Democratic Greek League (EDES) and its military wing (EOEA). He had approximately 150 men under his command and his operations were largely confined to the mountainous Epiras region. The other group would eventually become the National People's Liberation Army (ELAS), the military wing of the communist National Liberation Front (EAM) led by Aris Velouchiotis, whose true name was Athanasios Klaras. Velouchiotis's group was marginally larger than that of Zervas.

Back in Cairo, SOE needed to assemble a team. Lieutenant Colonel John Steven, an SOE planner, asked a headquarters staff officer, Edmund 'Eddie' Myers, if he knew of any parachute-trained sappers. Myers told him there were none in the Middle East; however, he was himself a 'sapper' – an engineer. The officer looked at Myers and asked, 'Well, what's that badge you're wearing?' Myers had only recently completed a short parachute training course at Kabrit in Egypt and was wearing his wings on his sleeve. One thing led to another and Myers was chosen as team leader, despite being a 'regular' soldier. Another 11 men would join him. Myers's second-in-command was Major Christopher 'Monty' Woodhouse, an experienced SOE officer who spoke fluent Greek and had already jousted with the Germans on Crete. The team was told that Woodhouse would remain in Greece after the raid while the rest would return to Egypt. It was to be a 'one and run' mission.

The team would be inserted into Greece by air in three groups by RAF B-24 Liberators from Egypt. Major Woodhouse's diary listed the make-up of the teams, each of which had a linguist, radio operator, sapper and team leader as follows:

First team: Colonel E. C .W Myers, Captain D. Hamson, Captain C. E. Barnes and Sargent L. Wilmot.

Second team: Major C. M. Woodhouse, Captain N. Barker, Captain A. Edmonds and Sergeant M. Chittis.

Third team: Captain J. Cook, Lieutenant T. Marinos, Lieutenant I. Gill and Sergeant D. Philipps.

On 30 September 1942, the aircraft lifted off from an airfield west of Cairo and turned north. The flight took about 4 hours. When the aircraft got to the drop zones there was a complication as the reception committees did not use the correct signals. One team was received by a group that was expecting supplies, not manpower, and were initially disappointed. It seems the main coordinator on the ground had been arrested and was the only one locally (other than the Prometheus II network) who understood exactly what the *Harling* mission was.

Only two teams jumped that night. The third team under Captain Cook could not locate their drop zone and returned to Egypt. They would arrive in Greece several weeks later. The miscommunication would delay the operation, and one guerrilla group, the EKKA under Colonel Dimitrios Psarros, inexplicably withdrew from participating in the mission despite having received one of the teams on the drop zone.

When Myers finally got his team together with that of Major Woodhouse he would have to find enough men to carry out the task. He dispatched Woodhouse to locate Zervas's group, while another officer went off to find Velouchiotis and persuade him to join the mission. While Zervas was enthusiastic, Velouchiotis – the communist – distrusted the British. It was only when he learned that his rival Zervas was involved that he agreed. At that point, the British did not understand that Velouchiotis and his guerrillas were leaning towards Moscow. It was a detail that would later lead to serious consequences for Greece.

Myers first conducted a reconnaissance of the three bridges and decided that the Gorgopotamos would be their target. Dropping it would mean at least several weeks of disruption to Axis rail movement. The Papadia was too open, while the Asopos was too difficult a target for the moment.

Myers planned the operation and decided to organise his assault force in seven groups. The Gorgopotamos viaduct was 200 metres long and spanned a deep gorge, which necessitated two separate teams to eliminate the guards at either end and protect the demolition party.

Two additional groups were tasked to block access to the area. They would cut the telegraph and telephone wires north and south of the bridge and carry explosive charges to break the rails and prevent the approach of any train bearing reinforcements. Another group of 30 ELAS men under the command of Woodhouse was held nearby as a reserve force. The final two groups were the demolition party of 17 men – Barnes, Cook, five other British soldiers and 10 guerrillas – who would carry and place the 350kg of explosives, and the party with Woodhouse, Zervas and Velouchiotis jointly commanding.

The teams moved into place and the raid launched only 15 minutes behind schedule at 11:15pm on the evening of 25 November.

The north end of the bridge was attacked by a combined group of ELAS and EOEA guerrillas; at the same time, the south end was assaulted by 30 EOEA guerrillas. The south side, held by around 75 Italians, was quickly suppressed while the north, held by only 25, took longer. A train approached from the direction of Lamia but the blocking team was able to blow the track and stopped the train from reaching the site.

Eventually Myers had to commit the reserves, but even then, the north end defenders held out. He was forced to send in the demolitions team with the battle still underway. Captain Barnes and his men took an hour to place the explosives on the central steel pier before he could give the signal for everyone to take cover. When the charges went off, three long spans of the bridge dropped into the gorge. A final explosion served to further damage the structure.

At 3:02am on 26 November, the withdrawal signal was given and the *Harling* force moved out of the area. The guerrillas suffered a few injured and wounded men, but none were badly hurt and the British team was unscathed. The Italians lost 20–30 men killed.

The next day, the local Italian commander executed 16 Greeks from the village of Lamia in retribution for the attack. The repair of the bridge took six weeks, and although it came too late to influence the crucial second battle of El Alamein, it totally disrupted communications between Athens and Salonika.

The action encouraged the guerrillas and the British alike. It was decided that Myers and his party would not return to Egypt. Instead they would remain with the Greeks and support their resistance against the Axis occupation.

> 'It showed for the first time in occupied Europe that guerrillas, with the support of allied officers, could carry out a major tactical operation coordinated with allied strategic plans.'
>
> – MAJOR MONTY WOODHOUSE

Support of Operation *Overlord* ... the JEDBURGHs

> 'A commander can more easily shape and direct the popular insurrection by supporting the insurgents with small units of the regular army.'
>
> – CARL VON CLAUSEWITZ, *ON WAR*

Long before the Allied invasion of Europe of 6 June 1944 got underway, intensive planning began for what would be one of the largest and most complicated military operations ever conceived. Soon after the evacuation of Dunkirk back in 1940, operations officers began to consider how best to return to the continent. An experimental assault was tried at Dieppe in August 1942 but was a costly failure, with 4,500 of the 6,000-strong force killed, wounded or captured. Despite its failure, lessons were learned, among them that landing at a well-defended port was out of the question and that concentrated naval gunfire support of the landing forces was vital. The British landings in Norway in April 1940 also provided valuable experience.

Although attention turned to the Mediterranean – Churchill's 'soft underbelly of Europe' – from 1942 until 1944, planning for a landing on the western coast of Europe continued. A final assault of Germany would be needed to destroy Hitler's Reich, and that assault would come through France.

The formal planning of the joint operation fell to a British officer, Major General Frederick E. Morgan, a veteran of World War I. Morgan was assigned as Chief of Staff to the Supreme Allied Commander (COSSAC) on 12 March 1943. He and 50 British, US and Canadian officers worked on the task. Morgan had been working on a British plan called *Round-Up* for a landing on the coast since 1941. Part of the planning process included how best to use unconventional forces to support large-scale combat operations. The plan for the invasion of Europe was renamed *Sledge Hammer*, later becoming *Overlord*.

SOE planners followed a train of thought initiated by 'Joe' Holland and L. D. Grand, who were working together temporarily in Section D in 1939, which posited that, 'If guerilla warfare is co-ordinated and also related to main operations, it should, in favourable circumstances, cause such a diversion of enemy strength as eventually to present decisive opportunities to the main forces.'

In May 1942, Brigadier Gubbins, SOE's Director of Training and Operations, wrote:

> A project is under consideration for the dropping behind enemy lines, in cooperation with an Allied invasion of the continent, of small parties of officers and men to raise and arm the civilian population to carry out guerrilla activities against the enemy's lines of communications. These men are to be recruited and trained by SOE.

Within SOE, Peter Allix Wilkinson, a close confidant of Gubbins, would be the principal architect for SOE's support to Operation *Sledge Hammer*. His original concept was:

As and when the invasion commences, SOE will drop additional small teams of French speaking personnel carrying arms for some forty men each. The role of these teams will be to make contact with local authorities or existing SOE organisations, to distribute the arms, to start off the action of the patriots, and, most particularly, to arrange by W/T communication the dropping points and reception committees for further arms and equipment on the normal SOE system. Each team will consist of one British Officer, one W/T operator with set and possibly one guide.

As previously discussed, this was the second phase of SOE's and OSS's mandate. The first phase building up to the Allied invasion of Europe started with SOE's first mission into France in June 1941. SOE was working closely with De Gaulle's exiled Free French government to assist the resistance aligned with him, as well as unilaterally with the 'non-aligned' resistance (but never the communists in France). There were a myriad of resistance groups in France, which bloomed into existence once the shock of German occupation wore off. SOE began on a small scale to build the circuits that would grow into full-fledged resistance forces, first by sending small teams of operatives into enemy territory by air or sea to organise, train and equip guerrillas to conduct operations against the Germans. Not all the groups were under Allied control, nor were their aims complementary. It was a complicated war on many fronts.

By the time OSS joined SOE in France in 1943, there may have been as many 2,500–3,000 resistance members in France alone. Beginning in the summer of 1943, OSS/SO infiltrated its first operatives, Francophone Americans or French nationals, into France. By 1944, 83 OSS Special Operations (SO) operatives were in the country helping to train and organise for the upcoming invasion.

Wilkinson's plan was to bolster the resistance with more than just radios and supplies. The teams would be able to advise and direct tactical offensive operations by the resistance behind the lines while staying in close contact with the conventional forces commanders to coordinate those actions to their best effect. They would be, in effect, a force multiplier that ensured the resistance operations added to the conventional, main force effort.

In July 1942, SOE/SO (later SFHQ) planners agreed that the plan would require at least 70 three-man teams to be inserted into France to assist the resistance forces. Liaison elements, called Special Forces Detachments, would also be required at each corps headquarters to coordinate the JEDBURGH activities once Allied ground forces landed on the continent.

The first step was to recruit specialist operatives for the three-man teams. Each team would be made up of one Francophone British or American officer, one French officer and a radio W/T operator, either a British, American or French NCO. The British soldiers came primarily from SOE, although some SAS troopers were included, while the Americans came from the OSS's SO division. The French mostly came from either the *Bureau Central de Renseignements et d'Action* (BCRA) or the French SAS Regiment.

The operation was given the random code name JEDBURGH, which happened to be the name of a Scottish village and meant nothing at all, except to the men who became part of the operation and called themselves 'Jedburghs' or 'Jeds'. The operation was headquartered at Milton Hall, about 90 miles north of London. The staff and men would live, train, sleep and prepare for their missions there. Unlike the members of the Operational Groups, the Jedburghs would wear Army uniforms and have no prepared cover story. (The OGs had the option of dressing in civilian clothing and thus risk being treated as a spy if captured. In any case, they would be shot either as a 'spy' or a 'commando'.)

The final arrangements for the plan would be worked out after a series of field exercises held in the United Kingdom, the first of which was in March 1943, exercise *Spartan*. Eleven teams took part and validated the overall concept, although adjustments needed to be made to how the teams reported information and the equipment they carried. Exercise *Dachshund* followed and ironed out additional issues on training requirements for the teams. Thereafter, several staff exercises were held to work out coordination issues between the liaison teams and the conventional headquarters.

More exercises were held in early 1944 that tested procedures on establishing contact with resistance groups in theatre and then coordinating and conducting operations against the enemy. The teams were considered operationally adept on their own, but required additional practice working with the resistance.

In March 1944, the specific teams were formed in a unique arrangement called 'marriage'. Essentially, the teams chose themselves based on their ability to work together well. Only occasionally would a team be broken apart by a 'divorce', and by April the teams were set.

In April, a six-day exercise, *Spill-Out*, was conducted to simulate conditions in France and bring together all the lessons learned. The final exercise was called *Lash*, and for 10 days the teams practiced communications and railway sabotage. It concluded on 8 June 1944, but several teams were pulled out of the exercise early for unspecified reasons, which would become clear shortly.

What would be the teams' targets? Generally, they were to conduct sabotage to blow bridges, damage factories and ambush enemy forces moving towards Normandy, particularly by rail, in order to disrupt any German counterattack against the invasion. In addition, some teams were tasked with 'counter-scorch' missions to prevent the demolition of key bridges by the Germans as they retreated.

The teams were hamstrung by a requirement put on them by General Dwight Eisenhower, the Supreme Allied Commander. Although supportive of the JEDBURGH mission, Eisenhower did not want to infiltrate the teams early to prevent a compromise of the D-Day invasion date. That restriction would limit the ability of some teams to successfully conduct their missions because the invasion force swiftly overran their operational areas. Others would have more than ample chances to assist the Allied forces.

The first JEDBURGH team, HUGH, jumped into central France on 5 June 1944. Then came HARRY on the 6th, with ISAAC on the 7th, QUININE and VEGANIN on the 8th and then FREDERICK, AMMONIA and GEORGE following them in on 9 June.

Typically, teams would be alerted several days before their actual insertion date and be brought to a briefing centre on Baker Street in London. There they would receive their orders, maps and be given photos and descriptions of the resistance contacts who would meet them on the drop zones (DZ) or they would have to search out and find. Team members would also be assigned code names that they would use in their radio transmissions.

HUGH

JEDBURGH Team HUGH was made up of French Captain Louis l'Helgouach, British SOE Captain William Crawshay and French W/T operator René Meyer. They were to be dropped in

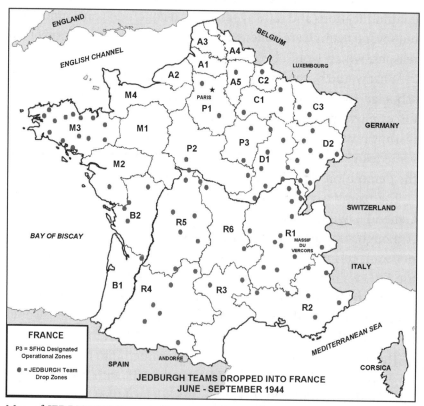

Map of JEDBURGH Team infiltration points and operational areas in France. (James Stejskal)

blind; that is, they would not be met on the DZ. Jumping in with them were two officers from a SAS team known as BULLBASKET. The SAS team was to set up a base called Samwest from which they could launch raids in the area to disrupt German attempts to counter-attack the Normandy bridgehead. In total, 55 men along with two armed Jeeps would be parachuted into the area over the following days.

OSS Lieutenant John K. 'Jack' Singlaub, JEDBURGH Team JAMES member, in full gear, armed with a M1A1 carbine and a 9mm Llama automatic pistol. (NARA, RG 226, Author's collection)

Team HUGH's mission was to assist to set up the base and to introduce the SAS to the local resistance. On 5 June, Team HUGH was transported to an airfield at Tempsford in Bedfordshire. After suiting up, they were inspected to ensure they weren't carrying any material that might be of intelligence value to the enemy. Each man was equipped similarly with an M-1 carbine, an automatic pistol (usually a Colt M1911A1), compass, survival kit, maps and rations to tide them over for several days. When they departed the airplane, several 'C' canisters would accompany them with radios, rucksacks and weapons for the resistance. Each member of the team also wore a money belt with several hundred thousand francs for dealing with the resistance and often gold coins for escape and evasion purposes.

They boarded a Halifax late in the evening and headed for France. By early morning, they were on the ground in the Chateauroux area of Indre and had made contact with the resistance. Their priority was to help the SAS cut the railway lines serving Limoges-Châteauroux and Bordeaux-Tours and prepare to receive two additional JEDBURGH teams, HAMISH on 12 June and JULIAN on 6 August, who would also operate in the area.

HUGH's operational area had been developed by two SOE 'F' section circuits, WRESTLE and SHIPWRIGHT, under the command of SOE officers Pearl Witherington and Amédée Maingard respectively. Because the resistance was well established, HUGH was able to get to work immediately. Reinforced by supply drops, they began to harass the Germans. As soon as the invasion began on 6 June, the resistance was flooded with volunteers. This made supply and security difficult – there weren't enough weapons for everyone and 'undesirable' elements fell in with the group.

It was not long before the presence of the SAS camp at Verrieres was discovered by the Germans, alerted by both French informants and the SAS's lack of security. The SAS team leader learned of the compromise and was about to move camp, but a battalion-sized SS armoured infantry element attacked them on 3 July. By early afternoon, 34 of the SAS troops were captured. They were forced to dig their own graves and executed by the SS.

Team HUGH learned of the German atrocity and requested a reprisal air raid on the headquarters of the 17th SS *Panzergrenadier* Division, the unit responsible. The RAF was quick to respond. On 14 July, 14 Mosquito fighter-bombers dropped high explosive and incendiary bombs on the unit's barracks during the evening meal. Between 100 and 200 SS troops were killed. The remainder of the SAS BULLBASKET group continued their activity, conducting 23 road and rail sabotage operations, until they were withdrawn back to England on 24 July.

A message from HUGH criticised the SAS team: 'This attack was mainly due to the lack of security shown by the SAS who, even at that early stage, paraded about the countryside in Jeeps.'

Inter-Allied Team returning to England after a mission in France. (492nd Bombing Group Files, US Air War College Archives)

HUGH continued its operations undaunted. By August, it had around 6,000 *Maquis* conducting raids and operations against the German forces in the area. One of the most important missions was to guard the bridges at St Brieuc, Guincamp and Morlaix to prevent the Germans from destroying them before Patton's Third Army arrived. This they did with 2,000 resistance fighters. By 10 September, HUGH was able to report its zone 'liberated'. Its last radio transmission was, 'Fighting was over, politics began, HUGH left.'

GEORGE

JEDBURGH Team GEORGE's mission was to assist a Free French SAS team called DINGSON to help the resistance disrupt German operations. Like HUGH, the intent was to harass, hinder and delay the Germans in the area to keep them away from the Normandy invasion zone.

GEORGE was dropped into the Morbihan department of Brittany in western France on 8 June 1944. Led by French Captain Phillipe Ragenau, along with US Army Captain Paul Cyr and a French W/T operator, 2nd Lieutenant Pierre Gay, GEORGE began to experience problems from the outset.

They were alerted for the mission at their base in England on 4 June and taken to London on 6 June for briefings on their task, the resistance leaders they would meet, as well as intelligence on the German forces known to be in the area. They were then taken to the despatch airbase, where they met SAS Commandant Pierre-Louis Bourgoin. Captain Cyr noted in his after-action report (AAR) that there were tensions with the SAS from the start. The SAS were unsure why they needed GEORGE's help, and it was only through Captain Regenau's conversations with the team that they started to understand and accept their presence.

The night of the drop, GEORGE and a small SAS advance party parachuted into France. Cyr later reported the flight over was like being packed in a sardine can. On the ground, they were met by a reception party from the *Bureau des Opérations Aériennes* (BOA) and taken to the camp area near Redon. The first problem began with communications – GEORGE was handicapped by two damaged W/T sets and constant radio jamming by the Germans. The SAS was still receiving supplies and men because it was operating on a separate net directly to its command in England.

GEORGE first met with their designated contact, an SOE circuit agent code named FERNAND. Through FERNAND and other contacts, the team began to alert local *Maquis* groups and men started to show up at the camp in droves. The shear mass of people arriving and leaving the camp was a big security issue, but the French were too exuberant to care much about security.

Unfortunately, DINGSON would meet a fate similar to BULLBASKET because it chose to stay too long in its base camp at Saint-Marcel. Over a period of several days after GEORGE arrived, over 100 SAS troopers were dropped in along with nearly a thousand containers of weapons and ammunition to arm the resistance.

Team GEORGE. (NARA)

Two additional French resistance operatives, HAUTEUR and FONCTION, began to assist GEORGE, which was just as well because once the distribution of weapons began, the *Maquis* began to shoot up German targets too close to the camp. The population reached critical mass when 5,000 *Maquis* were armed in the area; that many armed resisters alerted the Germans that they had a security issue.

Team GEORGE, in consultation with HAUTEUR and FONCTION, decided to move to another region, the Loire Inférieure, which was strategically important and, more importantly, very poorly organised. On 17 June, the night before their planned departure, another large air drop occurred and the SAS received four armed Jeeps, more weapons and explosives.

GEORGE's concerns were apparently mirrored by the Germans, who, having heard the massive airdrop, may have decided they had been invaded by an airborne unit. The actions of the French patriots also spiked German concerns.

On 18 June, there were 600–1,000 *Maquis* in camp when two German staff cars with *Feldgendarmerie* soldiers (military police) came in contact with a roadblock. The *Maquis* manning the checkpoint did what was natural, shooting up the Germans, but in the melee one escaped and alerted his headquarters.

Within an hour, all hell broke loose as 150 Germans, preceded by 25 civilians as cover, approached the site. The *Maquis* again opened fire and stopped the Germans, but they were soon reinforced by about 4,500 troops of the 275th Infantry Division, 2nd *Fallschirmjäger* Division and an *Osttruppen* unit made up of Russian deserters. At one point the SAS were able to divert some Allied P-47 Thunderbolt fighter aircraft covering the invasion forces and receive air support, which kept the Germans' heads down for about an hour, but the aircraft then left the scene.

The fight lasted from the early daylight hours until late that night before Commandant Bourgoin ordered the SAS and Team GEORGE to break out. Bourgoin had held on only because the camp was sitting on a valuable cache of 5,000 weapons that were to be distributed. Now he ordered the stores to be blown up and his soldiers to make for a rendezvous point several miles away. Captain Cyr and Ragenau both led *Maquis* companies out of the area.

'Carpetbagger' Squadron B-24 drops resupply container in a daylight run over France, June 1944. (492nd Bombing Group Files, US Air War College Archives)

At several points, GEORGE was surrounded by Germans searching for them. Because of the high grass and the number of people who had been in the area, the German tracker dogs were of little use. The Germans resorted to using grenades to try to flush out their quarry, but everyone kept quiet and stayed put, and eventually the Germans moved on.

By the end of the battle, around 600 Germans had been killed, with the SAS and *Maquis* losing 250 men. Eighteen SAS men were captured and later executed.

GEORGE split from the *Maquis* and the SAS and reconsolidated about 25 miles away to make its way cross-country to their new base. They journeyed on foot, staying in the forests or at farms known to be friendly. HAUTEUR and FUNCTION served as guides during the journey. They left one farm, only to learn later that the Germans had killed the owner when they determined he had aided their escape.

Eventually, they came to the village of Questembert. While the team remained hidden, HAUTEUR put on his civilian clothing and went into the village to find food. He met a friend who could help with transport, and they were able to use a farm truck to drive 75 miles to Saffre. It was a rather unpleasant journey as they were hidden among a load of rather odorous pigs.

At Saffre, they met a new *Maquis* group of 200–250 men who were waiting for arms. Almost immediately, the Germans attacked the camp. They were aware of the small camp but had thus far ignored them until they heard that a JEDBURGH team had joined the group.

Once again, they escaped across country and avoided their hunters, eventually making contact with a new resistance cell near Ancenis. Captain Cyr assessed this group and the region as a bad place for resistance because of numerous infiltrations by Gestapo agents and overall carelessness by the members themselves. They held meetings openly in cafes and made little effort to hide their associations. There was also no trust among the various groups, each of which had different motivations.

Amusingly, Cyr wrote that he had been dealing with four types of *Maquis* groups:

1. 'Political groups interested in the resistance' – these were like the communist *Front National* who were pursuing future ambitions.
2. 'Resistance groups interested in politics' (which he assessed to be a different thing) – these were the anti-communist group 'liberation and vengeance' and the communist FTP.
3. 'Political groups pretending to be interested in resistance but really only interested in politics' – among these were various groups under influence of political parties that constantly changed names.
4. 'Resistance groups not interested in politics' – these were Cyr's 'Angels', the groups only interested in getting rid of the Germans, such as the *Organization de la Resistance dans l'Armee* (ORA) and the military organisation of the department which was organised by de Gaulle's *Forces Françaises de l'Intérieur* (FFI) rules.

Unfortunately, each group suspected each other or wanted them out of the way and issued daily orders to 'kill the traitors'. Cyr opined that there were 'many Napoleons and many brave men, but no one knew who to obey' (*OSS Special Operations* (London), Vol. 1, Bk 4).

Team GEORGE, with the help of HAUTEUR and FUNCTION, took command as the official Allied military presence and got each group to agree on the principles of unity of command, agreed goals and no politics. Most importantly, there would be no more independent action, no '*Maquis Mobilisateur*' – self-actuating saboteurs who acted however and whenever they liked, without any coordination.

Captain Ragenau reluctantly became the *Délégue Militaire* for the region, and the team set out to train the men and improve security and morale. But they were still having communication problems, were receiving no supplies and they were broke. Since they had no money to pay the *Maquis*, who had no way to feed their families, they resorted to stealing money from banks. Still, they were able to sabotage rail lines, bridges and destroy two locks of the Brest canal (which marooned 20 barges of supplies for the Germans) using stolen explosives.

They moved again in early August to St Sigismond. There, the resistance presented them with the plans for the German U-Boat pens at St Nazaire and the coastal defence system, which had been copied by French engineers working with the German Todt organisation.

After reporting this windfall to London and receiving no answer, Captain Cyr was able to make the dangerous journey through the no-man's land between the armies into the American lines and pass the invaluable blueprints to VIII Corps. Cyr was sent on to Patton's Third Army headquarters. He was met by Colonel Powell, the SF liaison on Patton's staff, and explained GEORGE's communications predicament. Shortly thereafter, they received new radios and had arms and explosives (and cash) dropped to them for the first time.

They were given orders to re-establish order and security in the newly liberated areas and help the American Third Army in its flanking movement around Paris. While also conducting counter-scorch operations to prevent the German destruction of infrastructure, they arranged to guide the US forces as they advanced.

On 20 August, they received a message: 'Have urgent mission for Jed George ... send three London urgently with all radio equipment. Inform them all three been proposed for Croix de Guerre with Palm.'

The team's AAR chronicled its operations and problems with communications. Ironically, London thought GEORGE was being 'played back' by the Gestapo. Interestingly, GEORGE's radio 'finger print' was technically checked 'when messages received raised doubts as to the identity of the operator'. The record proved the original operator was still sending.

Despite that confirmation, HQ continued to believe GEORGE was sending under duress. The confusion was a result of the long delay between the team's insertion and their first radio contact, as well as misinterpreted security procedures by officers on the staff. It was only when Colonel Powell reported that he made contact with the team that the HQ reassessed their doubts (Source: TNA HS 7/34).

With hindsight, one might wonder why HQ did not ask the SAS team about GEORGE or why the team did not utilise the SAS radio net to communicate a message to their own HQ when they began to have problems.

Nevertheless, GEORGE persevered. Cyr proudly wrote in his AAR that, by 23 August, they had 2,500 uniformed men under arms protecting the right flank of Patton's Third Army from Radon to St Etienne, while harassing two German divisions around St Nazaire.

Team GEORGE II returned to France on the night of 8 September for its next mission. By the war's end, Phillipe Ragenau had been decorated with the Military Cross, Silver Star, Medal of the Resistance and Legion of Honour. Paul Cyr received the Distinguished Service Cross for the GEORGE missions and the Bronze Star for his service with OSS Detachment 202 in China.

Ninety-one additional JEDBURGH teams were dropped into France, with the last being inserted on 27 September 1944. Eight additional teams were dropped into the Netherlands, many to support the ill-fated Operation *Market Garden*.

The overall value of the 'Jeds' has been argued for many years. Some considered the effort too little, too late, while others thought the resistance forces assisted by the JEDBURGHs, Operational Groups and Inter-Allied Teams to have been well worth the effort. Not all the teams were successful: several were destroyed by the Germans. Team JACOB in the Vosges Mountains region, for example, was dropped into an area that was saturated with German counter-guerrilla forces and run to ground.

Some teams were dropped into the fray too late and were simply overrun by Allied forces before they could do much of anything. Many of the teams did have an effect, however, serving to delay counter-attacks, divert badly needed resources and harass the enemy behind their lines. Historian Don Lawson, in his book *The French Resistance*, estimated that their effort was the equivalent to that of 15 infantry divisions.

Perhaps the most succinct evaluation came from General Dwight Eisenhower, Supreme Allied Commander, in 1945:

> I consider that the disruption of enemy rail communications, the harassing of German road moves and the continual and increasing strain placed on the German war economy and internal security services throughout occupied Europe by the organized forces of resistance, played a very considerable part in our final and complete victory.

A Plateau Too Far: the Battle for the Vercors

The Vercors plateau in south-east France was always described as a fortress. It is a natural redoubt some 30 miles long by 15 miles wide, with towering walls on its outer margins and access limited to just a few roads. Historically, it had always been used as a hideout, and so it came naturally to the *Maquis* to select it as a bastion for its operations in 1942.

Unfortunately, it would serve as an example of the danger of concentrating irregular forces too early. By 1944, the *Maquis* were well on their way to fortifying the Massif du Vercors, a plan they called 'Montagnard'. The difficult roads up into the area were covered by armed parties and the resistance was confident in its ability to secure the plateau. But they did not have the heavy weapons – the mortars and artillery – necessary to defend the plateau, an ill-advised decision for guerrillas.

The overall intent of the plan was to support the eventual Allied landings in France by launching hit-and-run raids on the Germans to disrupt their rear areas and take some pressure off the landing forces. The *Maquis* also expected the Allies would reinforce them with airborne troops when the time came. But they showed their hand early by impatiently beginning to conduct small-scale attacks on the Germans in the spring of 1944. The Germans observed aerial supply drops and knew that more and more men were massing on

C-47 'Dakota' airdrop to a JEDBURGH Team. (CIA, Office of the Historian)

the plateau. The Free French command in Algiers instructed the *Maquis de Vercors* to declare the plateau 'Free' on D-Day, but the message didn't specify if that was for *Overlord*, the 6 June Normandy invasion, or *Dragoon*, the invasion of southern France, which was delayed to August. Algiers was also unaware that the plan for large-scale resupply and reinforcement had been cancelled.

On 6 June 1944, the BBC sent the message '*Le chamois des Alpes bondit*' (the chamois of the Alps leaps) – words that called them to action. The *Maquis* declared the Vercors to be a '*République libre*' and raised the French flag over all the plateau's villages. About 5,000 *Maquisards* from the plateau and surrounding region assembled. Openly jubilant, the *Maquis* were nevertheless still worried that they would not be reinforced soon enough.

In late June, two Allied teams were dropped in to assist the *Maquis*: the Inter-Allied mission EUCALYPTUS, led by SOE Major Desmond Longe and Captain John Houseman along with five men,

Photo taken from a fighter escort following a 'Carpetbagger' drop. French resistance fighters scramble to retrieve containers with weapons and explosives, circa June 1944. (492nd Bombing Group Files, US Air War College Archives)

and the OSS OG JUSTINE, led Captain Vernon G. Hoppers with 14 men. Both teams were infiltrated on 29 June to help instruct the *Maquis* on the weapons they would receive.

The first offensive action taken by the *Maquis* was an ambush on 7 July. Led by OG JUSTINE, a section of 20 *Maquis* they had trained and armed set an ambush on a main north-south route near the village of Lus-la-Croix-Haute. Their target was a German convoy of six vehicles and 120 troops. The ambush resulted in 60 dead and 25 wounded, with three trucks and one bus destroyed.

But the call to action was premature. The French command should have waited until Operation *Dragoon* was launched. For the moment, every resource was tied up with supporting operations in Normandy. The mobilisation order was countermanded, but it was too late.

Many messages were exchanged and the Allies finally responded on Bastille Day, 14 July, with a huge air drop of 860 containers of supplies – one source states over 1,500 containers were dropped. But the heavy weapons the *Maquis* had requested were not included.

The Germans had noted the airdrops and began to plan retaliatory action. The German regional commander of southern France, *Generalleutnant* Heinrich Niehoff, decided the massed resistance force was too dangerous to ignore; it was time to act.

Niehoff directed that operations should be carried out against the resistance headquarters. On 15 July, the offensive began with an aerial bombardment of the plateau that destroyed several villages. This was followed on 20 July by a full-scale assault that opened with attacks on the edges of the plateau by three German light and mountain infantry battlegroups, followed by an airborne assault on the plateau itself. The *Maquis* were surprised when 20 German DFS 230 gliders sailed onto the massif and disgorged troops from the elite *Luftwaffe* KG 200 squadron, along with *Sicherheitsdienst Einsatzkommando* (security service operational detachments). *Fallschirmjäger* (paratroopers) would join the fray the following day.

Violent battles took place over the next days, but the tide shifted rapidly in favour of the more heavily armed and better-supported Germans. All the *Maquisards* could do was skirmish and retreat. For the next four days, the resistance and the few Allied SOE and OSS operators among them fought a delaying action before escaping into the surrounding mountains. Led by the EUCALYPTUS Team, the *Maquis* attacked the enemy four times in three days, surrounded them completely and killed some 250 men. It is estimated that the 22,000-strong German force lost over 300 men, while the resistance suffered nearly 700 casualties. In addition, at least 200 civilians were killed either in bombings or executed by the Germans.

Vercors was an example of failure of command. Both the decision to mass troops openly and begin operations early, as well as the failure to support the region, resulted in needless loss of life and destruction of the *Maquis*. SOE historian M. R. D. Foot noted that

The mission of the Operational Groups (OG) in general was:

The OSS Operational Groups are organised to serve as the operational nuclei of guerrilla organisations which have been formed from resistance groups in enemy territory. They executed independent operations against enemy targets on orders of the theatre commander.

The aim of OG activity is to aid actual and planned Allied military operations by harassing the enemy behind his lines, by disrupting his lines of communication and supply, and by forcing him to divert troops to protect himself from guerrilla attacks and wide-scale uprisings.

– Operational Group Command Overview, OSS, 1944

Vercors violated the 'golden rule of the guerrilla: the task is to delay the enemy's passage over ground, not to hold it'.

Nevertheless, the Allied command put a bright spin on events. A SFHQ report summed up the action as having diverted elements of an armoured division, as well as ground troops, totalling an estimated 10,000 soldiers: 'The forces of the FFI thus were able to divert a considerable ENEMY force which might have been used elsewhere.' The SFHQ report apparently underestimated the size of the German force by half.

The Americans and Britons of JUSTINE and EUCALYPTUS escaped east. JUSTINE continued operations with the *Maquis* in the Belledonne Mountains and attacked a German force of 5,000 in early August, capturing 3,500 troops. Following the invasion of southern France, they met the advancing US Seventh Army near Grenoble.

The EUCALYPTUS Team was not as fortunate, being broken up during the assault on Vercors. Major Longe and Captain Houseman managed to escape to Switzerland, but most of the other team members were captured or killed.

Finishing Off the Stragglers: Operation *Rype* (OSS)

On 24 March 1945, eight 'Carpetbagger' B-24s lumbered off Harrington airfield in southern England and flew north. They would refuel in Scotland before heading across the North Sea towards their target: Norway's Jaevsjo Lake near the border with Sweden. On board were 31 men of the OSS's Norwegian Special Operations Group (NORSO) and four more from the Norwegian Independent Company 1. The team was under the command of Major William E. Colby and 1st Lieutenant Tom Sather, a former Norwegian seaman. Even though it was mostly an American unit, many were recent Norwegian immigrants to the United States who had been recruited from the US Army's 99th Infantry Battalion. Colby was not Norwegian, but he was an experienced OSS officer and already had one 'op' under his belt, having parachuted into France leading JEDBURGH Team BRUCE on 14 August 1944. Now, six months later, he was leading a bigger team with a specific purpose.

Each four- or five-man NORSO team aboard the airplanes had all they needed to create havoc: weapons, explosives, as well as their personal kit and, importantly, skis – the only way to get around the frozen Nordic landscape.

As usual for the time of year, the weather over Norway was treacherous. By the time the planes got to the intended area, only four could drop their teams. Two could not find the location and returned to base. Another dropped its five-man team in Sweden and they were immediately interned by the government. Those five would later rejoin the main group after a deal for their release was made with the Swedish security service.

Initially, only 20 of the 35 operators made it into Norway and were spread out over a 36 square-mile area. It took them several days to regroup. Supplies were also lost, some containers without parachutes burying themselves deep in the snow. Meeting the Norwegian 'MILORG' resistance on the ground went better, even though the Norwegians laughed at the challenge and password.

A member of OSS's Special Operations Group NORSO training for sabotage operations in Norway during World War II. He is armed with a Thompson sub-machine gun. (CIA, Office of the Historian)

They thought the phrase 'Is fishing good on the lake?' simply too foolish to answer.

According to Colby's unofficial report, their mission was 'to cut the Nordland rail line at two points in the North Trondelaag area. The purpose was to prevent German redeployment of 150,000 troops in northern Norway, which was being accomplished over these lines at the rate of a battalion a day.' If they could cut the highly channelled railway at the Grana bridge, the isolated forces would not be able to play a role in the defence of Germany.

But at that point, the OSS raiders were too few and would have to wait for more men to carry out their mission. Two more infiltrations were attempted, with the loss of two aircraft, their crews and 10 NORSO personnel. One of the planes crashed on 7 April within earshot of the team. A local reindeer herder informed them of its exact location and the team went out to recover the bodies and any equipment. (On 29 April, the team buried the 12 men at the site and rendered full military honours.)

Twelve days had passed without any action by the team, and several rather outlandish schemes to hijack and demolish a train were considered before an alternate to the Grana bridge was chosen. The new target would be a bridge in very difficult terrain near Tangen.

After skiing 35 miles to reach the target area, Major Colby gives a taste of just how difficult the trek must have been:

> The terrain was the most difficult I had ever seen. Picture the Hudson River, visualising the Palisades three times their true height. Place a railroad snug against the foot of the cliffs, and then crust the whole thing with four feet of snow and six inches of wet ice. Now, place 23 skiers atop the mountain, and they are carrying revolvers, tommy-guns, Garands, Brens, and 180 pounds of TNT plus other equipment on a massive sled. [Lieutenant Herbert] Helgeson [a Norwegian] said it would be impossible to get down. Men would break their legs, their skis. But I was a novice at skiing and knew motion is possible in positions other than upright. One patrol found an ice-logged waterfall that rambled in fairly easy stages in a deep, rock-lined gorge. It ended in the lake. Perfect, I thought. Mad, thought Helgeson.

On 15 April, the team descended the treacherous terrain on their backsides rather than attempt to ski down, except for Helgeson, who ended up breaking his skis. The bridge was unguarded because of its location, which made its demolition easy. After that, the team decided to sabotage the railway and took up positions along a 2.5km section of track. On 23 April, now reinforced by the returnees from Sweden, they blew the rail line with 240 separate charges of plastic explosive. Colby again details the action:

> The men fanned out for 2.5 kilometres and set the bombs. The plan was to detonate at 0005 on a green signal flare from me or, failing that, five minutes later. The nearness of an unsuspected German guardhouse prevented the flare plan and, at ten minutes past midnight, one tremendous crescendo rocked the valley. It was not one explosion here, one there, but the whole

works right on the nose. Frightening coordination. [Lieutenant Glenn J.] Farnsworth [team demolitions expert] had taught the men well. Then came the Germans like violated bees, shooting aimlessly into the air, setting off hundreds of flares. We ran. Someone fired at my team, but we ignored him. In the distance, a Garand rattled. It was Sather, hoping to get one of the hated enemy.

The team pulled back to a hideout along the Swedish border with a fair number of German ski troops in pursuit. Finally, in a base camp, five Germans stumbled upon them. Colby tried in vain to persuade them to surrender, but one of the Germans got off a burst from his MP-40 which hit a Norwegian guerrilla in the stomach. The team answered with a hail of .45 calibre ammunition from their Thompsons – the Germans' bodies were left for the wolves. The wounded man was dragged in a sled 50 miles into Sweden to a hospital. He survived.

The two raids reduced the German rate of troop movement south from one battalion a day to approximately one battalion per month. Some 100,000 German troops – 12 divisions – were trapped in Norway at the war's end.

The NORSO Team, notified after the fact of Germany's surrender, took part in policing 10,000 Germans at Namsos. It then acted as the honour guard for Crown Prince Olaf when he returned to Trondheim.

Colby and Sather were each decorated with the Silver Star, the others with Bronze Stars. Eleven members of the team were killed on the operation, all in air crashes. Colby would later serve as the Director of the Central Intelligence Agency (CIA).

In the Far East

In the Far East, SOE and OSS faced a number of obstacles and obstinate Flag-ranked officers that made operations difficult. For one, the defeat of Japan was of secondary importance to the Combined Chiefs of Staff. By agreement, Germany was to be the main Allied

Major Colby and his NORSO Team render honours to the crew and OSS members killed in a plane crash in the mountains of Norway. (NARA, RG 226)

target, which meant that men, money and materiel were devoted to that cause, reducing the military effort in Asia.

Even when operations were mounted, there were significant difficulties to overcome. There were no neutral countries through which clandestine intelligence operations could be launched against Japan. There were also problems finding personnel who could 'blend in' to the area – most Britons and Americans, being of other than Asian descent, could not operate openly there.

Another limitation was on the types of operations that could be mounted. In Europe, sabotage took precedence early on, with open guerrilla warfare only possible in conjunction with Allied conventional military operations such as the invasion of Normandy. In Burma and Malaya, the terrain and the enemy's extended lines of communication mitigated for guerrilla warfare. That said, the Far East was a long way from England and the United States, which made setting up and supporting missions difficult.

A final issue was the reticence of the Pacific theatre commanders to permit SOE and OSS operations in their respective areas of responsibility. This meant that both organisations were limited largely to the China-Burma-India theatre. To some extent, rivalry between Britain and the United States also hindered operations for the OSS. Burma was, after all, long in Britain's sphere of influence. While SOE was operating from India and Ceylon by 1942, OSS was just beginning to establish itself. Despite that, the Far East was the OSS's earliest operational deployment in World War II.

Mayhem and Propaganda behind the lines: Force 136 (SOE)

In March 1942, Force 136 was set up to organise 'stay-behind' resistance and psychological warfare (PW) operations in the Far East, the so-called CBI or China-Burma-India theatre. A section called 'Oriental Mission' was set up in Singapore, but the territory's capture by the Japanese ended that mission. A second element, initially named GS I(k), then 'India Mission', was established in Kandy in Ceylon (Sri Lanka). It was renamed Force 136 in 1944. Although missions were mounted in China, Thailand and Malaya, many of its operations took place in Burma.

In Asia, SOE operations were different from those run in Europe. There was no organised local resistance with whom they could work and the native peoples in the area generally did not like the Europeans, the result of years of colonial rule. There was also hostility between tribal groups within the countries. Here, like in Yugoslavia, SOE often had to align themselves with the few established underground forces, which were often the communists. Furthermore, SOE agents could not disguise themselves as locals and, therefore, relied on trained indigenous peoples to conduct reconnaissance and intelligence collection.

Force 136 conducted JEDBURGH-type missions, including Operation *Character*, which consisted of three-man SOE teams, including many Chinese-Canadians, who were dropped in to organise different tribal groups to oppose the Japanese in Burma.

The teams were especially effective working among the minority peoples of Burma, including Chins, Karens and Kachins. By war's end, *Character* was estimated to have raised an estimated 12,000 guerrillas. By agreement with the Americans, SOE focused its efforts on the Karen tribe, while the OSS worked primarily with the Kachins, however, in practice *Character* was a multi-ethnic organization. It was also one of the largest and most successful SOE operations of the war.

Operation *Character's* mission was to conduct operations in front of the British Fourteenth Army's advance into Burma in 1945, primarily in the Karen Hills of eastern Burma. Its specific tasks were:

- To keep Fourteenth Army informed about Japanese dispositions.
- To harass the retreating enemy, when called upon to do so.
- To keep under surveillance from the Karen Hills the road and railway running south from Pyinmana to Pegu.
- To observe the road from Toungoo in the Sittang Valley through the Karen Hills to Bawlake and Loikaw.
- To be prepared to oppose Japanese reinforcements coming up from the south or Japanese forces moving down from north and central Burma.

One element of *Character* was Team OTTER, commanded by a colourful character by the name of Lieutenant Colonel Edgar Henry William Peacock. At 51, Peacock was one of the oldest SOE officers in Burma, but he brought a wealth of experience, having worked with the Burma Forest Service for 16 years. He was working as an intelligence officer in India when SOE recruited him and was first deployed on the Chindwin Front in 'P' Force.

Peacock's service with OTTER is best described by his Military Cross (Bar) award citation:

> In March 1945 Lieutenant Colonel Peacock, after having been parachuted into enemy territory, raised and commanded a group of Karen guerrillas operating in the mountainous country north-east of PEGU. On 14 April he was warned that a Japanese division was moving along an axis running

SOE Force 136's Lieutenant Colonel E. H. W. Peacock of Team OTTER's Karen Guerrillas. (TNA HS 7/107 – Burma)

close to his base. The enemy's objective was to link up with the main enemy forces in order to deny us a vital airfield and communication centre. Within twenty-four hours Colonel Peacock had established a number of roadblocks. During the following ten days, by skilful handling of his guerrillas and a nicely timed series of demolitions, he succeeded in preventing the link-up of the Japanese forces. The objective was now in our hands. In this short period his guerrillas killed 114 of the enemy, destroyed a large amount of transport and blew six bridges. Credit for this outstanding performance must go largely to Colonel Peacock whose gallant leadership and sound tactical judgement have been important contributory factors in the success of the main operations. (TNA, WO 373/41/10)

His guerrillas were credited with 2,743 enemy troops killed, many more wounded and 94 vehicles destroyed, in addition to providing valuable intelligence to Army Headquarters.

One of Force 136's more unique missions was propaganda – efforts that included spreading rumours favourable to the Allied cause in the bazaars of India when the Allied military situation looked bleak. As circumstances improved, it was decided to send agents forward into the enemy-held regions of Burma to spread disinformation among the local populace and Japanese troops in advance of the planned Allied offensive called *Arakan*.

Several SOE infiltrations took place, including Operation *Mahout*, a mission to insert by parachute several Bengali communists to create unrest among dock and railway workers. The first was 'SDG', who parachuted into Burma in June 1943. He created a little disruption by sabotaging supplies before he began to sow discord among the coolies which caused some to quit their work. In September 1944, he was arrested, questioned and tortured by the Japanese until his release in March 1945. His experience was not unique but, happily, he survived to tell the tale.

In 1943, agent operations were augmented with forward propaganda elements called Indian Field Broadcasting Units (IFBU). Teams with native Japanese speakers (many from Korea) were infiltrated in enemy-held areas to collect intelligence and conduct propaganda operations behind Japanese lines. The IFBUs were made up of one SOE Officer Commanding and 56 other personnel, mostly drawn from the Assam Rifles. By January 1943, five units had been raised and committed, one in the Arakan region and four in the Imphal. It was soon realised the units were too small and they were reorganised to company size, with about 169 men under the command of an SOE major.

The units used loudspeakers and mortar-fired leaflet canisters to deliver propaganda messages to the Japanese, with some success, but one officer matter-of-factly stated 'the Japanese could not always be counted on to surrender'. On occasion, the units were engaged in direct combat with the enemy. In one encounter, 17 Japanese soldiers were killed and the IFBU commander was awarded the Military Cross (MC).

Captain Peter J. Goss, SOE, was posted to No. 2 IFBU and, in January 1945, his unit penetrated the area between the Chindwin and Irawaddy Rivers ahead of the 20th Indian Division as part of Operation *Barge*. Their mission was to collect intelligence and conduct a 'hearts and minds' operation to win over the locals.

SOE Team MONGOOSE, part of Operation *Character*, inspecting a train demolition near Kyaikto, carried out using 10lb of plastic explosives and a pull switch. (TNA HS 7/107 – Burma)

On 13 March, Goss commanded an armed escort accompanying a field propaganda section led by Captain Bacon. Bacon's section was to broadcast a call to surrender to an isolated group of Japanese. When the detachment approached to within 70 yards of the enemy, the Japanese opened fire with machine guns. Bacon and an Indian soldier were hit and badly wounded. Both were rescued by Goss, who ran forward under heavy fire and carried them individually to safety. Goss was recommended for an MC, but in the event was mentioned in despatches. At 20 years old, he was one of the youngest SOE officers in Burma (HS 1/192, WO 373/92).

The operation lasted four months, and the IFBU were among the first Allied troops to reach Rangoon on 2 May.

Force 136 operations were essential to the successful evacuation of British forces from Burma in 1942, and then crucial to protecting Field Marshal William Slim's right flank as he advanced back into the country in 1945.

'Count these and divide by two' – Kachins and Detachment 101 (OSS)

The first COI/OSS operational unit to reach Asia was also its first complete operational unit to be dispatched overseas. The twenty-one original members of Detachment 101 (Det 101) established their base at Nazira in Assam, India, in May 1942 and began operations shortly thereafter. This was only two months after the fall of Rangoon to the Japanese and the British withdrawal of its forces from Burma into India.

Understanding that the British wanted OSS under its control, Lieutenant Colonel Garland Williams, the Director of COI Special Activities Group (the forerunner of OSS/SO), named the unit 'Special Unit Detachment 101', saying he wanted to confuse outsiders about how many such units existed. Before the unit could even be deployed, COI director Donovan expended much personal capital with US Army General Joseph Stilwell to get it into the CBI theatre. Donovan had already been rejected by General Douglas MacArthur and Admiral 'Bull' Halsey, who did not want any part of OSS in their realms, respectively the South-West Pacific theatre and South Pacific area. In World War II (and even today), some American commanders had serious misgivings about unconventional warfare and the units that used such 'undisciplined' methods.

Donovan (and his deputy Millard Preston Goodfellow) managed to convince Stilwell of the need for OSS. Stilwell saw a requirement that could be fulfilled by Donovan's men, but it wasn't in China where he was located; it was in Burma. US Army Colonel Carl Eifler was given command of the unit, and after weeks of training at Camp X in Canada and in the Catoctin Mountains of Maryland, the outfit deployed to India. Officially activated on 14 April 1942, it was the first American unit ever assembled to conduct guerrilla warfare, intelligence collection and sabotage behind enemy lines.

General Stilwell was preoccupied with reopening the Ledo or 'Burma' road, the main overland supply route across the mountains to China. Because of the Japanese, the road had been closed and

SOE Captain Peter Goss behind the lines in central Burma with No. 2 IFBU of Force 136, holding a captured Japanese flag, March 1945. (Courtesy of the Peter Goss family and the SF Club)

supplies going to China had to be flown in from India. The Japanese were able to shoot down many of the cargo planes from an airbase in northern Burma at Myitkyina. Stilwell wanted Eifler's men to deny the Japanese the use of Myitkyina airport and the roads and railway leading into it from the south, and prevent supplies from reaching the base. That would mean going behind the lines to collect information and cut the roads and rail lines. Stilwell's oft quoted admonishment to Donovan was, 'I don't want to see you again until I hear a boom from Burma.'

From their headquarters at Nazira (ostensibly an experimental malaria research site), Det 101 launched its first forays into enemy territory. Long-range reconnaissance missions were attempted, but failed. Eifler lowered his aim a bit and began to run short-range missions. The method of insertion changed from foot infiltration to parachute drops. Small teams of Americans working with the

Kachin tribesmen began to spread out over the region – some of the most difficult terrain and inhospitable climates possible.

The Kachin were well-suited for the mission. Extremely hostile to the Japanese, who had made the mistake of trying to dominate them by fear and inhumane treatment, they were physically tough and mentally at home in the jungle. Most importantly, they were natural hunters who could move silently and knew the ground well. Eifler's force began to train them in sabotage techniques, while the Kachin taught their new friends how they liked to set up ambushes.

By early 1943, the detachment began to run operations deeper into Burma. The first took place in February, when Captain Jack Barnard and a team of Burmese agents jumped into the Kaukkwe valley of central Burma with the mission to cut the Mogaung-Katha railroad and then organise guerrillas south of Myitkyina. The team successfully destroyed a railway bridge, but heavy Japanese patrolling forced them to scramble out of the area. Det 101 had two failed missions that paused operations for a while, but they were back in action before long, providing Stilwell's headquarters with 'jungle telegraph' intelligence on Japanese activities and locations. According to David Hogan's *US Army Special Operations in World War II*:

> [The unit] developed a general operating scheme that it used repeatedly in support of the Allied advance into Burma. Before the detachment could organise guerrillas in a given area intelligence and prior contacts were essential. From forward bases near the combat zone the unit infiltrated, by air or foot, small teams of advance agents behind Japanese lines to reconnoiter and locate friendly natives. For the most part, the detachment arranged reception committees for the agents; only rarely did they enter an area blind. Once the agents reported favourable conditions, combat cells, including Americans, parachuted into the areas and established operating bases to recruit and train guerrilla bands and to undertake a series of hit-and-run attacks against Japanese installations and outposts. After conventional or guerrilla operations had finally driven the enemy from the area, the forward headquarters advanced into the region, and the process repeated itself. The guerrillas generally operated from 50 to 150 miles behind enemy lines; advance agents deployed about 100 to 200 miles beyond the guerrillas.

Early in 1944, Det 101 was called on to support Stilwell's ambitious plan for an advance into Burma, with more guerrilla warfare and less 'hit and run' sabotage. Donovan decided on some changes, and Eifler, suffering from head injuries incurred on an operation, was replaced as commander by William R. 'Ray' Peers.

As part of the offensive, Det 101 would screen the flanks of the US Army's 5307th Composite Unit (Provisional) under Frank Merrill (aka 'Merrill's Marauders') as it moved towards Myitkyina. The Marauders were directed to flank the Japanese 18th Division as Stilwell's Chinese main force slowly advanced from the north-west. The advance would end in a long, bitter siege for the Marauders at Myitkyina.

During the campaign, which lasted from February until August 1944, Det 101 provided guides and porters, collected advance intelligence, harassed enemy outposts, cut communications lines and ambushed enemy convoys, all of which enabled the 5307th to complete its mission. Det 101's reporting stated simply that they conducted 'all operations which they [regular forces] are not prepared to undertake'.

Although the Myitkyina campaign was long and hard fought – Stilwell would be severely criticised for his failure to properly resupply and support Merrill, as well as his delay to ask for British assistance – Det 101 was able to help ensure the eventual Japanese defeat. During the advance and siege, the Americans and Kachin of Det 101 broke up every Japanese attempt to counter-attack. But it was only with Chinese and British forces – the 'Chindits' under Brigadier Mike Calvert – that Stilwell's force was finally able to break the siege. The Japanese commander was finally forced to order the withdrawal of his forces, and then, dishonoured, he committed *seppuku* – ritual suicide.

From August to December 1944, Det 101 supported the Allied advance to a phase line from Katha to Bhamo and, by January 1945, they had reached Lashio. There, two battalions of Kachin raiders transitioned from Phase 2 guerrilla warfare to Phase 3 conventional combat operations and destroyed 1,000 well-entrenched Japanese defenders, albeit at a high cost. The Burma road, closed since 1942, was finally reopened in March 1945. The Japanese in Burma surrendered in Rangoon on 28 August 1945.

Through the campaign, the 100 Americans and 10,000 Kachin raiders of Det 101 were responsible for 5,500 confirmed Japanese killed, with 10,000 more reportedly wounded or killed, as well as 57 bridges and 272 vehicles destroyed, and the rescue of over 400 Allied airmen. The unit was also responsible for 85 per cent of the intelligence supplied to Northern Combat Command and 75 per cent of the targets provided to the Tenth Air Force. The unit was disbanded on 12 July 1945 and received the Presidential Unit Citation on 17 January 1946.

The story goes that General Stilwell once sceptically asked a Kachin leader about the Japanese whom he said he killed, 'How can you be so sure of the numbers?' The Kachin dumped a bunch of ears from a bamboo tube into a pile on Stilwell's desk and said, 'Count these and divide by two.'

Planned but Never Carried Out

War often brings out rather outlandish or strange ideas of how to quickly bring an end to conflict. Nowhere was this more evident that in some of the plans thought up and nearly put into operation by SOE and OSS during World War II. One idea was to go straight to the top to kill the supreme leader – *Der Führer* Adolf Hitler himself.

Foxley (SOE)

Perhaps it was because of the 'success' of SOE's Operation *Anthropoid* that the British high command thought it might work. Or perhaps it was just an exercise, a conceptual *Kriegspiel* meant to 'red team' an operation before it was proposed.

Whatever the origin of the plan, *Foxley* was the name given to SOE's planning and preparation for an eventual assassination of

Adolf Hitler. The idea was first pushed forth sometime during 1944, when an SOE officer was tasked to answer two questions:

1) Is killing Hitler desirable?
2) How could it be accomplished?

Located in the files of TNA (HS 6/624) are the *Foxley* papers, which lay out in great detail the concept of how the assassination could have been carried out. The primary location considered for the operation was at the Berghof, Hitler's Bavarian retreat in the Obersalzberg outside Berchtesgaden. An alternate possibility was the *Führerzug* – Hitler's armoured train used to travel between Berlin and Berchtesgaden.

It was surmised that operatives could get access to the train at the Salzburg train station sidings and poison the potable water tanks which served the *Führer*. At the Berghof, a number of options were studied, including a sniper attack on Hitler during his daily walk. A second possibility was to use a bomb or anti-tank rocket launcher to kill him in a vehicle.

Obviously, the attack was never carried out. Whether the first question was answered is not known. The second question is answered with a basic concept that might have served as a basis for the operation. The biggest problem was the target himself – after the 20 July 1944 attempt on Hitler's life by his own troops at the *Wolfsschanze* near Rastenburg in East Prussia, Hitler rarely travelled. The assassination team would most likely have had a long wait.

Iron Cross (OSS)

The British were not the only ones who wanted Hitler dead. As the Soviet Army neared Berlin, the Americans thought Hitler would escape and fall back on the so-called *Alpenfestung* or Alpine Redoubt in the Bavarian Alps. William Donovan decided on a plan to capture Hitler there. It was called *Iron Cross*.

American Captain Aaron Bank, a Jed who had jumped into France with Team PACKARD, was chosen to lead an advance team of four

Target: Adolf Hitler. Hitler thought photos of himself in shorts undignified, so he banned them. (Peter Wickman/Public Domain)

men in German uniforms to locate Hitler either at the Berghof or elsewhere in the Alps. Once Bank's team located Hitler, a follow-on volunteer force of 100 German Army troops (former prisoners of war) would be parachuted in to conduct the capture.

The team was assembled at Dijon, France, in April 1945 and was prepared to launch, but the mission was delayed six times before it was finally cancelled. Ironically, it was another OSS operation, *Greenup*, which collected the intelligence that the *Alpenfestung* was just a fantasy of Heinrich Himmler's. Bank would go on to be the first commander of the newly established US Army 10th Special Forces Group in 1952.

What would have happened had either of the above missions been carried out is an intriguing enigma.

Allies become Enemies

With the capitulation of Italy, Germany and Japan, the SOE and OSS were thrust into new territory. Teams who had completed their missions were pulled back to their home bases, where they turned in equipment and completed the required war diaries and AARs that make up a unit's history and leave lessons learned for those that followed and cared to read them. (Historians love AARs, but for the most part they would not be permitted to read the classified reports for many years.)

Other operatives were sent off on new missions made necessary by the end of the war. Several teams were parachuted into areas where POW camps were known to exist after the Axis capitulation to protect the prisoners from last-minute execution by their now-defeated and possibly vengeful captors. These 'mercy missions' usually entailed the formalisation of surrender terms – sometimes facing off against an armed enemy guard force that was not prepared to give up – and then providing immediate care to the prisoners so they could be evacuated to friendly territory.

In several cases, SOE or OSS officers made direct contact with enemy commanders who wanted to negotiate the surrender of their troops before their leadership was inclined to do so. This was more often than not the Italians and some Germans, as the Japanese were disinclined to surrender without the Emperor's permission.

A major issue in post-war Europe was the deactivation of the guerrilla armies. In Norway, Belgium and Holland there were few issues. In France, however, there were many problems. Fragmented politically and humiliated after its 1940 surrender to Germany, most French citizens wanted a change of government and punishment for the Vichy collaborators. Although de Gaulle's government ordered the resistance to disarm, many did not. The communists felt it was their time for power, as did the right-wing partisans. This began a period of crisis for the Fourth Republic that lasted for many years and began the unravelling of the French Empire. It would soon lose Algeria, then Indo-China. The same peoples who helped free France and its colonies from German and Japanese occupation now fought to free themselves from France itself.

Italy's transition from war to peace was smoothed somewhat because it became a co-belligerent against Germany following its armistice with the Allies in September 1943. Nevertheless, there were teething pains as the royal house of Savoy tried a comeback but was defeated in a referendum that ended the monarchy. What followed was a struggle between the communists and other parties. The Catholic Church and covert action by the CIA managed to limit the Italian communist party's influence, however.

In the Balkans, Stalin began to erect a curtain of satellite countries as a defensive buffer against the West to protect 'Mother Russia'. Poland, Hungary, Bulgaria, Albania, Romania, Czechoslovakia, the Baltic States and eastern Germany fell under the Soviet sphere of influence. Yugoslavia went its own way under Tito.

SOE and OSS had initially supported the Chetniks, but then switched to backing Tito for the remainder of the war. By the time they departed Yugoslavia, OSS had 15 teams supporting Tito's forces, while SOE had at least 14 teams in the country. The Yugoslavian underground did its part, forcing the Germans to commit 15 divisions and 100,000 local troops to suppress their activities.

The price for this support was that Tito, aided by the Soviet Army, consolidated power by eliminating Dragoljub Mihailović's Chetniks and ensured the communists gained and retained complete control after the war. Although communist, Tito broke with Stalin and maintained Yugoslavia as a non-aligned country. Tito's actions may have been influenced by his contacts with the British and Americans who advised and assisted his partisan movement.

After the withdrawal of German forces in 1944, Greece was wracked by conflict as the forces of the right and left clashed for control of the government. In December 1944, EAM (communist) forces moved against the British-installed interim government. The brief but violent revolt was quashed by British troops, only to reignite as the Greek Civil War in 1946, with the communists being supported by Tito (but not Stalin). Many have blamed SOE (and OSS) for arming the resistance during the war – forces who opposed the monarchy and who propelled Greece into the rebellion. Most historians agree, however, that British Foreign Office policy to reinstate the King of Greece was incompatible to fighting the occupation and was further confused by Churchill's directive to work with any group that opposed the Axis. The conflict in Greece would last until 1949, with its political acrimony continuing even longer. The Allies may have given the groups their weapons, but the will to fight among themselves was ever present.

In the Far East, the political situation changed radically for the former colonial powers of France and Britain, while the Americans would encounter new friends who would become new enemies.

Hồ Chí Minh and Special Operations Team DEER (OSS)

The OSS's record in South-east Asia and China was mixed. Det 101's mission in Burma was a success, while operations throughout the rest of the region were just getting off the ground when the war ended. In French Indo-China, the OSS was only able to deploy teams in the spring of 1945.

One was called Team DEER. Led by US Army Major Allison Thomas, it had been dropped into the jungle near Tan Trao, not far from Hanoi. Their mission was to contact the local guerrillas and train them to fight the Japanese, specifically to cut the rail line between Hanoi and Lang Son – the route to China. Like Det 101, they were also to report on enemy targets and local weather that would help the Air Corps to launch missions.

The operation had become necessary when the Japanese finally seized full control of Vietnam from the Vichy French colonial administration. In so doing, they cut off all communications out of the country, including the Free French agents in place. The OSS knew of a Vietnamese man who could help, a man who went by the pseudonym Mister 'Hoo'. Hoo had recently travelled to China to bring a downed American pilot back to his comrades. Hoo said he would be happy to accommodate an American team into his guerrilla band. More than ridding Vietnam of the Japanese, Hoo wanted American assistance to help him to expel the French and set up an independent republic. From the French, the OSS knew Hoo was a rebel, anti-French and a communist. But the OSS pragmatically decided that if Hoo could do the job, they would use him.

Key to the agreement was that Hoo wanted to meet the pilot's American commander. That was the Fourteenth Air Force's General Claire Chennault. He asked for a signed photo of Chennault to take home with him. As it turned out, that photo would be essential for Hoo to establish his leadership of the revolt. Hoo helped a small American team set up in his camp in the summer of 1944. They would send out intelligence information to the Fourteenth AF, but by 1945, more intelligence and, most importantly, more action against the Japanese was needed. That was where Team DEER came in.

Thomas went in on 16 July 1945 as the leader of the 'Pilot Team', a three-man advance element that would assess the guerrillas' potential and needs, as well as give the follow-on team information to assist their preparations. First Sergeant William Zielski accompanied Thomas as the W/T operator, along with interpreter Private Henry Prunier. Landing on the designated DZ, they were met by several hundred local fighters of the *Việt Minh*, the League for the Independence of Vietnam. They were introduced to their leader, Mister 'Hoo'. Hoo was in reality Hồ Chí Minh and his military commander was another interesting personality, Mister 'Van', aka Võ Nguyên Giáp.

The rest of the team that joined Thomas on 29 July consisted of Lieutenant René Defourneaux, Staff Sergeant Lawrence R. Vogt, Sergeant Aaron Squires and Private Paul Hoagland, the medic. They set about the task of training the guerrillas on modern firearms (M-1 rifles, 60mm mortars and bazookas) and small unit tactics, the tactics they would use on the Japanese, and then their arch-enemy, France. The first priority for the team was to save Hồ's life. Told that he was sick, Hoagland visited Hồ and determined he was suffering from any one of a number of jungle afflictions. Hoagland's treatments of quinine and sulfa drugs may well have saved Hồ's life.

Team DEER spent August training around 50 recruits until 15 August 1945, when they heard of the impending Japanese surrender. The team was advised to turn their weapons over to the Vietnamese and return to China. Shortly thereafter, Hồ formed the National Insurrection Committee. Among the items Hồ displayed at the meetings were pictures of Mao, Lenin and his signed photo of Chennault, which intimated American support. He signed documents 'Nguyen Ai Quoc'; a man the French thought dead but who was well known to them as a Comintern agent trained by the infamous Soviet operative Mikhail Borodin.

His small, newly trained force marched towards Hanoi with Giáp in command. It encountered a Japanese fortification at Thai Nguyen on 20 August and attacked. Major Thomas, despite being ordered not to participate, was present and giving advice. Some have assessed this operation as a test of the force that was to demonstrate psychologically and politically the combat capabilities of Hồ's outfit, but also prove that he and Võ Nguyên Giáp were capable leaders of the coming rebellion. The Viet Minh seized Hanoi on 19 August and began to consolidate the North. Then, on 2 September 1945, Hồ Chi Minh declared the independent Democratic Republic of Vietnam. Soon, a new war would grip the country.

With the exit of the Japanese, French colonial power returned to Vietnam and the nationalists' calls for independence were ignored. France was seen to be a necessary bulwark against communism in the coming Cold War. Letting France keep its colonial possessions would ensure it stayed with the West and, later, NATO when it was established. The inroads made with Hồ as an independence-minded nationalist were soon lost amid fears of communist expansion and belief in the domino theory.

When Major Thomas sat down to his farewell dinner with Hồ, he asked the diminutive, wispy bearded revolutionary if he was indeed

OSS DEER Team, 1945. L–R: Unknown, Rene Defourneaux, Hồ Chí Minh, Allison Thomas, Võ Nguyên Giáp, Henry Prunier, unknown, unknown, and Paul Hoagland; kneeling: Lawrence Vogt, Aaron Squires, and unknown. (NARA, RG 226)

a communist. Hồ answered, 'Yes. But we can still be friends, can't we?' One wonders.

Communists in Malaya – SOE and the MPAJA

SOE trained Malayans to oppose the Japanese during World War II. They supported, among others, the communist-sponsored Malayan People's Anti-Japanese Army (MPAJA), which was composed mainly of ethnic Chinese guerrillas against the Japanese. It was a relationship that would turn problematic when the time came to demobilise.

During the war, Force 136 operated in Burma, Malaya, China and Thailand. Its operations in Malaya have had much scrutiny because of the role played by the successor of the MPAJA, the Malayan Races' Liberation Army (MRLA), in the Malayan Emergency from 1948–57.

SOE's Oriental Mission attempted to recruit and train Malays before they were forced to evacuate Singapore, but their efforts were hindered by the British command in Malaya who felt the idea was impracticable. Nevertheless, some SOE operators remained in Malaya with their 'students' as stay-behind forces. Many SOE operations after the fall of Singapore were run from Ceylon or Australia – missions that were difficult to launch and sustain because of the distances involved.

In 1941, with the anticipated arrival of the Japanese, communist cadres in the cities withdrew to the countryside to prepare to fight the occupation. They were predominantly organised by the Malayan Communist Party (CPM) and, as usual, many of their members were already trained in subversive warfare. By 1943, the MPAJA consisted of eight battalions, with 10,000 men in the jungles of Malaya and operatives inside the urban areas.

From the beginning, SOE's relationship with the CPM and MPAJA was mutually beneficial, but some saw problems in the future. According to Malaysian Army Major Shamsul Afkar bin Abd Rahman, 'The end game [would be] the communist insurgency against colonial Britain.'

With the surrender of the Japanese, the MPAJA came out into the open. It repudiated the agreements made during the war and kept most of the arms it had been provided with. It soon declared its political aim to be independence from the British and to establish the 'People's Democratic Republic of Malaya'. In 1948, many communists left Singapore for the Federation of Malaya, and from there mobilised many MPAJA veterans into a new force: the MRLA. Conflict broke out once again. The British government declared a state of emergency and began to fight a counter-insurgency against a force it had taught to be guerrillas just a couple of years before. The Malayan Emergency lasted another 12 years, but that, as Kipling would say, is another story.

The Russians Are Not Your friends: Captain Stephanie Czech Rader (OSS)

Stephanie Rader was born in Toledo, Ohio, in 1915 to Polish immigrant parents. She was raised in Poughkeepsie, New York, and only spoke English at school. In 1937, she received a degree in chemistry from Cornell University. When the war began, she joined the Army and was selected for Officer Candidate School. Quickly promoted to captain, Rader was soon recruited by the OSS because of her foreign language skills and sent to London for operational preparation. She deployed to the American Embassy in Warsaw, Poland, in September 1945 as an operative assigned to the OSS's X-2 branch.

OSS Captain Stephanie Czech Rader wearing Women's Army Corps branch insignia. (US Army, NARA, RG 226)

In late 1945, after the OSS was disbanded, Rader was absorbed into the War Department's short-lived Strategic Services Unit (SSU), where she continued her intelligence work. By that time, Poland was very much under the thumb of the Soviet occupation forces. Living day-to-day under the watchful eyes of the NKVD was by no means easy.

As the only Polish-speaking operative in the embassy, Rader worked under the cover of a clerk and spent her spare time travelling throughout Poland, ostensibly searching for long-lost relatives. While on these trips to the far reaches of the country, she collected information on Soviet troop concentrations and movements as well as on the Polish security service – the *Urzad Bezpieczentwa*. She was also able to report on economic conditions and political data where the US Embassy had no other access to information. During one visit to southern Poland, she actually found relatives and spent time with them while collecting strategic information of great value.

The US Ambassador tasked Rader to courier information back to Berlin, and, completing that trip, she was given sensitive information to take back to Warsaw. By that time, Rader knew that her cover had been compromised by a US official in Paris, but she continued with her mission. As she approached the border checkpoint, Rader surmised she would be arrested and searched by the Soviets. Before she reached the checkpoint, Rader was able to pass the documents to a person she travelled with and give instructions on how to deliver the materials later. She was indeed arrested, but, finding nothing, the Soviets were compelled to release her. The documents were recovered as planned.

Despite the fact that she was suspect and under constant surveillance, Rader chose to remain in place and finish her assignment. Rader retired as a major but received no special recognition for her work until her death in 2016 at the age of 100, when she was posthumously awarded the Legion of Merit.

When Rader finally left Warsaw, it was 1946. A new threat was on the eastern horizon – the Cold War had begun.

CHAPTER 5

The End of an Adventure

The end of SOE and OSS was not subtle at all, although little was said publicly in the case of SOE's demise. Churchill had been replaced by Clement Attlee as PM. When he was informed of the priceless network the organisation had at its disposal, Attlee was unimpressed. He said he had no wish to oversee a British Comintern and demanded it be shut down in 48 hours.

Colin Gubbins, although honoured with an appointment to the Order of St Michael and St George, was retired at his permanent or substantive rank of colonel rather than as a major general, his wartime rank. He went on to make his fortune in textiles while trying to ensure his former 'troops' were cared for. He founded the Special Forces Club in London as a meeting place for those who had served in the SOE and for veterans of similar organisations like the OSS.

SIS picked up many of the SOE officers it deemed suitable for its operations. Those who had run-ins with the organisation during the war were not invited to join. SIS also took in SOE's records and may still have some locked away, while those deemed safe enough for public viewing have been released to TNA.

Sir Colin McVean Gubbins, KCMG, DSO, MC, died on 11 February 1976.

In the United States, the OSS lost its main supporter when FDR died. Shortly before the President passed away, Bill Donovan presented him with a paper calling for the establishment of a permanent centralised intelligence organisation. The paper was

Spirit of Resistance memorial plaque. (Courtesy of the Special Forces Club who
retain the copyright. Photo: Ruth Sheppard)

leaked, possibly by FDR himself to test the waters, and Walter
Trohan, a journalist for the *Chicago Tribune,* scotched the plan
as 'creating a super Gestapo'.

When President Harry S. Truman was briefed on the plan, he
decided to forgo Donovan's idea completely. He issued an Executive
Order in September 1945 which abolished the OSS. The analysts of
the Research and Analysis (R&A) section went to the Department
of State, while the Counterintelligence (X-2) and Secret Intelligence
(SI) sections went to a new, temporary element called the Strategic
Services Unit. It would quietly become the Central Intelligence Group
(CIG) in 1946 and be the keystone of the Central Intelligence Agency
when it was established under the National Security Act of 1947.

OSS Congressional Gold Medal – sculptor Renata Gordon, designer Emily Damstra. (U.S. Mint)

Major General William J. 'Wild Bill' Donovan resumed his law practice and dabbled in the diplomatic world, becoming the US Ambassador to Thailand for a time. He died on 8 February 1959.

Many of the men and women of OSS would go on to serve in the new organisation, the CIA, while many would return to their military positions. Aaron Bank, along with others, would be instrumental in creating the US Army Special Forces – the equivalent of the OSS's Operational Groups.

Truman and the OSS

President Truman, like Henry L. Stimson before World War II, did not trust intelligence agencies. He reportedly told Donovan on 14 May 1945:

> I am completely opposed to international spying on the part of the United States. It is un-American. I cannot be certain in my mind that a formidable and clandestine organization such as the OSS designed to spy abroad will not in time spy upon the American people themselves. The OSS represents a threat to the liberties of the American people.

He would later change his mind, after the dissolution of the OSS, and set into motion the establishment of the CIG, the predecessor of the CIA.

Epilogue

'They gave back to people in the occupied countries the self-respect that they lost in the moment of occupation.'

– M. R. D. FOOT

There is a valour that often goes unrecognised. It is the quiet, desperate courage of the warrior who serves alone or in small groups in faraway, unknown places. They lead a life that might be ended by a bullet in the jungle or a garrotte in a cold basement cell, their fate never recorded in a report or obituary. Often they see no medals or reward beyond the satisfaction of knowing they've done their part for freedom. It is a valour that exemplified the operatives of SOE and OSS the moment they volunteered for duty.

Beyond that dedication and courage, however, the question must be asked: 'Was it worth their sacrifice and effort?'

SOE and OSS were set up at the beginning of the war to address a gap in strategy: essentially the lack of an army to fight the enemy on the continent. It was hoped that resistance in Europe (and elsewhere), along with naval blockades and strategic bombing, would bring about the defeat of the Axis. That was most true before the entry of the United States into the war. David Stafford, in his influential analysis of the resistance, *Britain and European Resistance, 1940–45*, asserts that the SOE was born out of Britain's desperate situation in 1940 and a belief in German susceptibility to indirect methods such as economic pressure and subversion. There was faith placed on a programme that would not always play out as envisioned.

Early in the war, British leadership hoped that resistance forces, aided by supplies and advisors, would rise up and defeat their oppressors, with British landings required only to assist the uprisings. In the end, it was the other way around – a direct confrontation between Allied and Axis forces would be necessary. From the point when the United States and Soviet Union entered the war, the resistance forces, and by extension SOE and OSS, were no longer central, but secondary and subordinate to the final strategic plan.

Despite Churchill's exhortations to 'set Europe ablaze', the contributions made by both organisations varied greatly across all theatres of combat. The sparks that the Prime Minister wanted to see start a conflagration were held in check by the realities of aircraft shortages, supply difficulties and the challenges that resistance groups faced as they tried to organise themselves and survive under hostile security control measures.

There was another issue that slowed operations: the Allied leadership, especially the British Foreign Office, who wanted to control the eventual political outcome at the war's end. Many historians and political scientists assert that the Allied leadership 'saw political dangers on the left' and sought to minimise those resistance groups to protect the pre-1939 status quo. As the Allies moved onto the offensive in the later stages of the war, SOE and OSS activities often became a source of conflict between strategic necessity and political post-war interest.

There was also animosity from other organisations like the SIS and Military Intelligence, who saw SOE and OSS as amateurs and interlopers who interfered with or endangered their intelligence operations. At the same time, that may have been a convenient excuse for their own failures.

Beyond the political, strategic and organisational issues brought about by their existence, SOE and OSS were created as a tool, a military – or more precisely para-military – option in the armamentarium of Britain and the United States. But as Lord Selborne of the Ministry of Economic Warfare noted: 'Underground warfare was an unknown art ... lessons had to be learned.'

What we can say with certainty from the outset is that on its own, guerrilla warfare, or whatever term is used to describe it, did not cause the Axis to collapse, Churchill's expectations notwithstanding.

As with almost any new undertaking, there were failures as well as successes. An action that was celebrated as a major coup by SFHQ in London might have been regarded as a mere nuisance by the enemy. Other operations, like the assassination of Heydrich, left a hole in the enemy's leadership that could not be made right.

Probably the most difficult missions were those involved in setting up and running the 'circuits', especially in France. The first individuals and teams were dropped into a situation that was often unclear. They had to work with underground groups that had varying degrees of aptitude in conspiratorial behaviour and security. Some circuits survived, but many were broken up over the three years of occupation before the Allied invasion began. At one point in 1942, a year after the first SOE infiltration, none of the circuits were operational, all having been rolled up by the Germans.

While there were many pinpricks of sabotage, the most important contribution of the resistance and their SOE and OSS enablers was the provision of intelligence which helped plan the strategic bombing raids and assisted the invasions of North Africa (*Torch*), Sicily (*Husky*), Normandy (*Overlord*) and southern France (*Dragoon*). OSS deception teams also fooled the Germans and diverted them away from Patton's successful late December 1944 counter-attack during the battle of the Bulge. Ironically, the US First Army had earlier failed to anticipate the surprise German offensive partially because it had banned the OSS from operating in its area of operations.

The volume of intelligence provided prior to the invasions by operatives on the ground was assessed to be a major factor in their success. SOE and OSS probably sent over 1,000 agents into France, and that was before over 300 JEDBURGHs and Inter-Allied Team operatives were infiltrated into France beginning on 6 June 1944.

There were great coups, like the Vemork heavy water sabotage and the major bridges destroyed in Greece and Italy. Military-oriented operations like Abyssinia (begun by MI(R) but completed by SOE), Yugoslavia and Burma were also quite successful. Conducting operations in Poland and Czechoslovakia was more difficult because of the distances from England. Worse, in Poland the resistance groups had two enemies: the Germans and Stalin's NKVD, who wanted to ensure there were no groups hostile to the Soviet occupation after the war.

As to their contributions to the Allied victory, there are many opinions. Would there have been the internecine squabbles in Yugoslavia, Greece, Italy and Malaya after the war had SOE and OSS not assisted the partisans or communist resistance groups? Or would there have been reprisals for assassinations and sabotage without the complicity of the British and Americans? The answer to both these questions is 'yes'. There were many examples of unilateral action that caused reprisals, and the political conflicts that began after the Axis downfall were already well in play even before the war started.

Most importantly, before D-Day both SOE and OSS provided a backbone of support to the local resistance groups that helped lift them in a moment of despair. Would they have done well without the support? Maybe, but probably not as well as they did. The resistance looked to the British and the Americans to provide them with the tools and advice which made the difference to their movements. By all accounts, the Italians and Germans dreaded moving through the countryside because of the threat the resistance posed to their wellbeing. The Japanese had a similar experience in their occupied territories.

As Germany crumbled in the final days of May 1945 and thereafter, SOE and OSS also played key roles to find and recover German personnel and secrets that would play important roles in the coming Cold War. They were also instrumental in recovering downed pilots during the war, and POWs in the days and months after the war to ensure they returned home safely.

Overall, their operations contributed greatly to the success of the Allied effort to win the war and hold the peace.

Glossary

AAR	After-Action Report
Abwehr	German Military Intelligence Service
ACP	Automatic Colt Pistol
AFHQ	Allied Force Headquarters
agent	a recruited field operative directed by an intelligence service
aka	also known as
Andartes	Greek resistance fighters (*Andartis* = singular)
Auxiliary	the support wing of a resistance or partisan movement
BCRA	*Bureau Central de Renseignements et d'Action* (established 17 January 1942)
BOA	*Bureau des Opérations Aériennes* – BCRA circuits to set up aerial resupply drops
BSC	British Security Coordination, New York
C	Chief of SIS, code name after Captain Sir Mansfield Smith-Cumming
CBI	China-Burma-India
CD	Director of SOE
CIA	Central Intelligence Agency
CIG	Central Intelligence Group, forerunner of the CIA
Circuit	SOE/OSS name for a team attached to an underground network
CO	Commanding Officer

COI	Coordinator of Information
CoS	Chiefs of Staff
CQB	Close Quarter Battle
D	'Destruction', SIS Section for sabotage
DF	direction finding
DMI	Director of Military Intelligence
DMO	Director of Military Operations
DNI	Director of Naval Intelligence
DoD	Department of Defense
DoS	Department of State
DSC	Distinguished Service Cross
DSO	Distinguished Service Order
DSS	Director of Strategic Services – William Donovan
DZ	drop zone
EAM	National Liberation Front – Greek communist resistance
EDES	National Democratic Greek League – republican resistance
EH	Electra House, Foreign Office affiliated propaganda section
ELAS	military wing of communist EAM
EM	enlisted men
EMFFI	*État-major des Forces Françaises de l'Intérieur* (French Forces of the Interior)
EOEA	National Groups of Greek Guerrillas, military wing of EDES
ETO	European Theatre of Operations
FBI	Federal Bureau of Investigation
FDR	Franklin Delano Roosevelt
FFI	*Forces Françaises de l'Intérieur* (French republican resistance organisation)
FN	*Front National* (French communist resistance movement)

FO	Foreign Office
F-S	Fairbairn-Sykes
FTP	*Francs-Tireurs et Partisans* (French communist resistance force)
Führer	'Leader' – Adolf Hitler's title after August 1934
GC	George Cross
Gestapo	*Geheime Staatspolizei* – Secret State Police
GS(R)	General Staff (Research): the first name for MI(R), see below
Guerrilla	member of a small independent group taking part in irregular fighting
HE	High Explosives
HQ	Headquarters
ISRB	Inter Services Research Bureau (cover name of SOE)
JCS	Joint Chiefs of Staff
JEDBURGH	Multi-national, three-man SO teams, usually American, British and French soldiers
LRDG	Long Range Desert Group
LZ	landing zone
Maquis	nickname for French rural Partisans
Maquisards	A member of the *Maquis*
MC	Military Cross
MD1	Military research and development section, formerly MIR(c), aka 'Churchill's Toyshop'
MEW	Ministry of Economic Warfare
MID	Military Intelligence Directorate (G-2)
MILORG	Norwegian Resistance Group
MI(R)	Military Intelligence (Research), initially GS(R), set up to study irregular warfare
MIR(c)	MI(R)'s research and development office, later MD1
MI5	Military Intelligence Department 5 – internal security and counter-intelligence
MI6	External Intelligence – see SIS

MI9	Military Intelligence Department Section 9 – Escape & Evasion Networks
MO	Morale Operations Branch
MO1(SP)	Cover name for SOE
MoD	Ministry of Defence
MTB	Motor Torpedo Boat
MTO	Mediterranean Theatre of Operations
MU	Maritime Unit
NARA	National Archives and Records Administration
NATO	North African Theatre of Operations, later MTO
NKVD	People's Commissariat for Internal Affairs, forerunner of the KGB
NCO	non-commissioned officer
NPS	National Park Service
OCI	Office of the Coordinator of Information
OC	Officer Commanding
OG	Operational Groups
ONI	Office of Naval Intelligence
Operative	fully trained individual employed by SOE or OSS, sometimes called an agent
OR	other ranks
OSS	Office of Strategic Services
OWI	Office of War Information – official 'white' propaganda service
PCO	Passport Control Officer
Partisan	member of armed group to fight secretly against an occupying force
Pétainist	collaborator
PID	Foreign Office Political Intelligence Department
PM	Prime Minister
POW	prisoner of war
PWE	Political Warfare Executive

R&D	Research and Development
RAF	Royal Air Force
RDX	Research Department Explosive
RE	Royal Engineer
RN	Royal Navy
RTU	returned to unit
SAB	Students' Assessment Board
SAS	Special Air Service
SBS	Special Boat Section
SD	*Sicherheitsdienst* – the intelligence service of the SS
Section D	SIS section 'Destruction', formed for sabotage operations
SF	Special Forces*
SFHQ	Special Force Headquarters, coordinating office at SHAEF, replaced SOE/SO
SHAEF	Supreme Headquarters Allied Expeditionary Forces
SH-200	German code name for heavy water
Singleton	operative or agent working alone
SIS	Secret Intelligence Service
SMG	sub-machine gun
SO	Special Operations
SO1	SOE propaganda section
SO2	SOE active operations section
SO3	SOE research section
SOE	Special Operations Executive
SOE/SO	Allied special forces coordinating office at SHAEF, later SFHQ
SOM	Special Operations Mediterranean, coordinating office at AFHQ
SS	*Schutzstaffel* – the armed corps of the Nazi party
SSU	Strategic Services Unit
STS	Special Training School
S&T	Schools and Training branch

TNA	The National Archives – Kew
Underground	group or movement organised secretly to fight an existing regime or occupying power
WO	War Office
W/T	Wireless Telegraphy
X-2	OSS Counter-intelligence branch

* Special Forces is capitalised in the US to designate a specific US Army unit, while the general term 'special forces' as used in the UK is usually written in lower case.

Select Bibliography

SOE Records (HS 1, HS 6, HS 7, HS 13, HS 15), Kew: TNA

OSS Records (RG 226), College Park: NARA

Burian, Michal, Knížek, Aleš, Rajlich, Jiri and Stehlík, Eduard, *Assassination: Operation ANTHROPOID, 1941–1942* (Prague: Ministry of Defense, 2002)

Chambers, John W., II, *OSS Training in the National Parks and Service Abroad in World War II* (Washington, DC: US National Park Service, 2008)

Duckett, Richard, *The Special Operations Executive (SOE) in Burma: Jungle Warfare and Intelligence Gathering in WW2* (London: I. B. Taurus & Co., 2017)

European Theater of Operations United States Army Historical Division, *The French Forces of the Interior: Their Organization and Their Participation in the Liberation of France, 1944*, microfilm, (Washington, DC: Library of Congress, Photoduplication Service, 1945)

Foot, M. R. D., *SOE: An Outline History of the Special Operations Executive 1940–46* (London: The Folio Society, 2008)

Hogan, David W., Jr, *US Army Special Operations in World War II*, CMH Publication 70-42 (Washington, DC: Department of the Army, 1992)

Irwin, Will, *The JEDBURGHs: The Secret History of the Allied Special Forces, France 1944* (New York, NY: Public Affairs, 2005)

Linderman, Aaron R., 'Reclaiming the Ungentlemanly Arts: The Global Origins of SOE and OSS', dissertation submitted to Texas A&M University (May 2012)

Linderman, Aaron R., *Rediscovering Irregular Warfare: Colin Gubbins and the Origins of Britain's Special Operations Executive* (Norman, OK: University of Oklahoma Press, 2016)

MacKenzie, William, *The Secret History of SOE: Special Operations Executive 1940–1945* (London: St Ermin's Press, 2002)

OSS Staff, *Assessment of men; selection of personnel for the Office of Strategic Services* (New York: Rinehart, 1948)

Strategic Services Unit, History Project, *War Report: Office of Strategic Services, Volume 1, Washington Organization* (Washington DC: USGPO, 1949)

Strategic Services Unit, History Project, *War Report: Office of Strategic Services, Volume 2, Operations in the Field* (Washington DC: USGPO, 1949)

Troy, Thomas T., *Wild Bill and Intrepid: Donovan, Stephenson, and the Origin of CIA* (New Haven: Yale University Press, 1996)

Acknowledgements

This book is dedicated to all those who fought against tyranny during World War II.

I am grateful for the assistance and advice provided for me by former Special Forces Lieutenant Colonel Will Irwin, author of *The Jedburghs*, Dr Richard Duckett, author of *The Special Operations Executive (SOE) in Burma*, and John Andrews, chairman of the Special Forces Club.

As usual, Ruth Sheppard and Isobel Fulton, the editors at Casemate Publishers, provided their professional advice, assistance and patience.

Most importantly, I thank my wife, Wanda, for her support, encouragement and understanding.

Index